The Modern Novel
in America
1900-1950

TWENTIETH-CENTURY LITERATURE IN AMERICA

GENERAL EDITORS

WILLIAM VAN O'CONNOR, PH.D.
University of Minnesota

FREDERICK J. HOFFMAN, PH.D.
University of Wisconsin

Fifty Years of American Drama, 1900–1950
by ALAN S. DOWNER, *of Princeton University*

The Modern Novel in America, 1900–1950
by FREDERICK J. HOFFMAN

Achievement in American Poetry, 1900–1950
by LOUISE BOGAN, *poet and critic*

TO BE PUBLISHED IN SPRING 1952

The Rise of Short Fiction in America,
1900–1950
by RAY B. WEST, JR., *of the University of Iowa*

An Age of Criticism, 1900–1950
by WILLIAM VAN O'CONNOR

Men, Ideas, and Judgments:
American Non-Fiction, 1900–1950
by MAY BRODBECK, *of the University of Minnesota*
JAMES GRAY, *of the University of Minnesota*
WALTER METZGER, *of Columbia University*

The Modern Novel in America

1900-1950

Frederick J. Hoffman

University of Wisconsin

HENRY REGNERY COMPANY

CHICAGO: 1951

100501

Copyright 1951

HENRY REGNERY COMPANY

Chicago 4, Illinois

Manufactured in the United States of America

CONTENTS

To
E. C. *and* C. E.

PREFACE

THE MODERN NOVEL IN AMERICA *examines the history of the twentieth-century American novel in terms of the two primary issues involved in its progress. On the one hand, there is the point of view largely emphasized by Henry James of "the art of fiction." The opening chapter discusses James's preoccupations with technique and method, together with their implications for the development of a critical aesthetic of the novel. One other principal issue, largely defined by the naturalists at the turn of the century, concerned the social relevance of a novel's materials, its philosophical grounding in a view of man and society, and the consequent discussion of a novelist's social responsibilities. The second chapter is largely concerned with this issue. Once these two tendencies have been established, this book examines the American novel of 1900 to 1950 in the following divisions: the work of Willa Cather and Ellen Glasgow and the influence of James upon each; the contribution made by Gertrude Stein to the art of those novels written after the first World War; the novelists of the 1920's, with detailed attention paid to the work of Ernest Hemingway and F. Scott Fitzgerald; the two widely separated points of view in the fiction of the 1930's, indicated under the heading "violence and rhetorical purpose"; and, finally, a consideration of the novels of the 1940's, as these show both a continuation of developments seen earlier in the century and the introduction of new or newly perfected skills and insights.*

In the course of the book, the major concern has been to study the effect of the novelist's attitude toward his materials (his aesthetic and his social views) upon the formal method used and its consequence for the realization of character, narrative sequence and pace, and setting. Many quotations are provided as crucial instances of the novelist's success or failure in realizing a formal result from the materials available. In this sense, the book is both a survey and a critical study of its subject.

A research grant for the summer of 1950 from the University of Wisconsin Graduate School helped considerably by providing needed time for the writing of this book. The author is also greatly indebted to Professor William Van O'Connor and to Philip Starbuck and William Strube for many valuable suggestions.

F.J.H.

March 15, 1951.

HENRY JAMES, W. D. HOWELLS, AND THE ART OF FICTION

WHEN Frank Norris said scornfully, "Who cares for fine style! . . . we don't want literature, we want life," he suggested a division in fiction which most of his contemporaries gladly accepted. Somehow, they thought, the strength of a novelist's value might be measured by the amount of "raw life" present, the amount of "fine style" absent. This division marks an important tendency in modern American literature generally, in fiction certainly. Style was in itself regarded as a defeating circumstance, and concern over style postponed, if it did not literally abandon the hope for, a direct approach to life. Life in this case meant society in the large: human nature muscular, glandular, and undressed—"scientific objectivity" which kept up to date with scientific discovery and experiment. There was a stimulating excitement in all of this; Norris' naturalist contemporaries could not be condemned for lack of courage or earnestness. They were in the thick of the fight against timidity, reticence—for "the Truth" writ large and splashed with color.

Of a temperament so precise and meticulous that it seemed a stranger to the naturalist group, Henry James quietly devoted himself to a quite different view of life and of the responsibility of art to it. James set out to reveal the state of a civilization, to study it in terms of the most highly conscious and discriminating intelligence he could bring to it. But for him the question of a civilization was reduced to a matter of individual sensibilities in close interaction and in subtle social intercourse. As Morris Roberts says of him, "He is . . . in a sense the most intellectual of critics, and yet the least interested of all in general ideas." Except for occasional acknowledgments of them, James did not invoke general ideas in his criticism; when he did (as in the case of his long essay on Zola in *Notes on Novelists*), it was primarily to show that science in itself (or philosophy, for that matter) did not necessarily bring us nearer life and might even keep us apart from it.

In short, James was a vital link in the continuation of the traditional novel, whose principal sponsors in the nineteenth century had been English. As an American writer, he also continued the American art of the novel, established chiefly by Hawthorne. The very extremity of his devotion to form in the novel not only served quietly as a minority voice in the naturalist clamor; it gave rise to, and somewhat emphasized, a very small body of criticism in the field of literature hardest to discuss as art and most readily available to anything but critical analysis.

That this was no empty "art for art's sake" interest was a fact that few critics or novelists were willing to acknowledge. His qualified dismissal of Flaubert's art, and his qualified admiration for Zola's "sincerity, passion for truth and seriousness of intention" should certainly have suggested that he was not interested in style per se, as opposed to the naturalist's life. He was concerned, not to discover how far art might dissociate itself from that life, but to determine just what the art of fiction formally involved and required. In the years 1906 to 1908, James worked on the project of a selected reissue of his novels and tales, the "New York edition." In the course of this work, he not only revised the fictions themselves, but proceeded to write a discriminating review of the formal problems their original writing had posed. The prefaces to these twenty-six volumes, combined with essays on the novel and on novelists, in *Notes on Novelists* (1914) and elsewhere, form an illuminating, and what amounts to a pioneering, body of critical investigations and principles for the art of fiction. It was to stimulate (though not always to dominate) the production of a small group of books dedicated to a similar purpose: Edith Wharton's *The Writing of Fiction* (1925) and Percy Lubbock's *The Craft of Fiction* (1921), among them; and in the revival of critical study in recent years, it was James who was invoked more often than any other as a guide and an acute critic of the art.[1]

[1] We may note especially the volume by Caroline Gordon and Allen Tate, *The House of Fiction* (1950), whose discussions of structure and point of view owe much to a continuing interest in James's critical writings. Other textbooks in the art of fiction include *Understanding Fiction*, by Cleanth Brooks and Robert Penn Warren (1943 and 1950); *The Art of Modern Fiction*, by Ray West and R. W. Stallman (1949); and *The Story: A Critical Anthology*, edited by Mark Schorer (1950). Among the magazines especially interested in the art of fiction, *The Western Review*, edited by Ray West at the University of Iowa, and *The Sewanee Review*, edited by John Palmer, are perhaps the best.

[From the beginning, James insisted that art in fiction served primarily to order life; life itself he called a "splendid waste," and it was only through the novelist's art that the significant and essential form might be brought to a realization of it: ". . . in literature we move through a blest world in which we know nothing except by style, but in which also everything is saved by it, and in which the image is thus always superior to the thing itself."[The controlling factor in the art of fiction is *method*, and James had always a vivid sense of the art-process, of the larger structural concerns which must at least begin the writing of a novel, and control both its scope and its enumeration and use of details. This is a primary distinguishing feature; it is through this fundamentally larger concern that James was able to mark the limits of such an otherwise distinguished talent, that of Flaubert. Style in Flaubert, his keen sense of the precisely relevant, did in his case serve to conceal the poverty of his subject. James was also able to see quite clearly the way in which facts exercise their tyranny over the artist when the material dominates him. The excessive passion for facts, or the refusal to see them as material upon which the process of selection and ordering works, can lead to fiction in which method has all but abdicated. So, in his review of "The Modern Novel," James gives credit to a chosen few, among them Edith Wharton and Joseph Conrad, for having discriminated and applied a method to their materials, for having approached them as conscious artists and not as mere obedient servants.

[One requirement which method imposes is that of the point of view—through whose eyes and intelligence the thing seen is actually given. The greatest contribution of James to modern fiction is his discussion and use of what he has variously called the "large lucid reflector" and the "central consciousness." Thus the range of the novel's *don-née* is seen in terms of the character who provides its point of view. The situation of a novel and the decisions that this situation requires, are after all the responsibility of those characters who are forced to face, to examine, and to act in terms of the situation. "I could think so little of any situation that didn't depend for its interest upon the nature of the persons situated and thereby on their way of taking it," he said in his preface to the New York edition of *The Princess Casamassima;* and some years earlier, in the now quite famous essay, *The Art of Fiction,* he had set aside such criticism which insisted on arbitrary divisions of "story," "incident," "character," by asking: "What is character but the determination of incident? What is incident but the illustration of character? . . . It is an incident for a woman to stand up with her hand resting on a table and look out at you in a certain way. . . ." For a character in a novel of James, doing and feeling are one, the interacting parts of a single whole; the action is itself qualified by the feeling toward it; the feeling is absorbed in determining the nature of the action. It may very well be that the action is slight, or even that it does not occur at all. In any event, the control which a point of view exercises upon the probabilities of action immensely and splendidly qualifies our awareness of them: "What a man thinks and what he feels are the history and character of what he does."

Under these circumstances of perception, it follows that the novelist will not seek necessarily for large actions and huge panoramas for their own sakes. The range of a central consciousness may be circumscribed so that his perception gains in subtlety of consideration and application. In fact, the novelist's concern ought not to be the canvas but the character—the discriminating intelligence of that central consciousness who is to make a situation artistically real to the reader. The fineness of a story's insight into whatever "scene" is indeed the fineness of its central character. This is not a trick of technique, but the very core of a novelist's moral view of his art. Granting willingly the success with which Flaubert had held his novel within the range of Madame Bovary's point of view, James nevertheless demurred with respect to the results obtained from that point of view. The central consciousness must be "richly responsible" and "finely aware" as Morris Roberts usefully puts it, "Its fineness creates the predicament upon which the story hangs, and in dealing with this predicament the character's lucidity and passion play upon and intensify each other; awareness heightens responsibility, and both are supposed to lend a high dramatic value to conduct by making it difficult and precarious."

In fiction and in the criticism of fiction, these matters of central consciousness and point of view opened a large area of discussion. James was himself to ring many changes on the notion. In one case, that of crucial dialogue, he was to transform fiction into a modified drama—notoriously in *The Awkward Age* (1899). In *What Maisie Knew* (1897), he was to show the subtly qualifying effect of a point of view—in this case, that of an intelligent child in an awkward situation—upon a subject (divorce) which he admitted was in itself sordid and ugly. In many instances, he was to supplement points of view by introducing the confidant or confidants, who have a varying but always a minor importance in the novel. Most skillfully, as in *The Portrait of a Lady* (1881), the confidant Ralph Touchett might eventually prove to be a character not only to advise and to see but actually to dominate the moral tone of a novel. But the use had its own risks; the confidant was too often irritatingly drawn in because a central consciousness could not give a completely satisfactory view either to the reader or to himself. Mrs. Wharton's remarks concerning the Assinghams of *The Golden Bowl* (1904) are perhaps an extreme indictment of this device:

This insufferable and incredible couple spend their days in espionage and delation, and their evenings in exchanging the reports of their eaves'-dropping with a minuteness and precision worthy of Scotland Yard. The utter improbability of such conduct on the part of a dull-witted and frivolous couple in the rush of London society shows that the author created them for the sole purpose of revealing details which he could not otherwise communicate without lapsing into the character of the mid-Victorian novelist chatting with his readers of "my heroine" in the manner of Thackeray and Dickens. Convention for convention (and both are bad), James's is perhaps even more unsettling to the reader's confidence than the old-fashioned intrusion of the author among his puppets. . . .

ii

The crucial facts of James's place in modern American fiction are two: the first, discussed above, is his concentration upon method and form in a world where these were usually touched upon only incidentally. The second may be said to have had a more immediately cogent effect upon the novel's history. It involved a difference of view over what precisely was to be known as the moral sense or the moral purpose of the novel. This was not dissimilar to the question of "literature and life" which Norris and others had raised. It was really a matter, not of affirming or denying responsibility to society, but rather of defining the precise nature of that responsibility. Hamlin Garland had insisted that a novelist could do no more or less than portray truthfully and honestly conditions which a politician might conceivably move to remedy or improve. The majority of book reviewers of James's time, and of Howells's as well, continued to assert a didactic purpose—perhaps the novel was not a moral fable, but it ought at least to show without too much subtlety or confusion the proper balance of virtue and moral sanction. Even if it criticized convention, it should remain basically conventional, which is to say, Christian and discreet. More pertinently, the "social novel" might also deal with social issues—that is, it might show characters more in external conflict than in inner distress. What nobler purpose than to demonstrate the degree to which American democracy had abused its original virtues, or had been abused by small but powerful minorities? From James to Howells to Herrick, there was a growing social sense, a movement away from subtlety to large purpose; the concluding scenes of Howells's *A Hazard of New Fortunes* (1890) lead by perceptible degrees to the direct and uninhibited social uses of the novelist's art found in Henry Fuller's *The Cliff-Dwellers* (1893) and Robert Herrick's *The Common Lot* (1904). These novels differ essentially from naturalist studies of society in the location of the critical intelligence engaged in the treatment of issues—in this case it was an upper-middle-class, "liberal" intelligence, remote from James's but equally remote from that of Dreiser, Upton Sinclair, or James T. Farrell.

That James was quite capable of using social issues and their determining doctrines can be seen in such novels as *The Princess Casamassima* (1886) and *The Bostonians* (1886). Lionel Trilling has said of these two works: "In these novels James is at the point in his career at which society, in the largest and even the grossest sense, is offering itself to his mind with great force. He understands society as crowds and police, as a field of justice and injustice, reform and revolution. The social texture of his work is grainy and knotted with practicality and detail. And more: his social observation is of a kind that we must find startlingly prescient when we consider that it was made some sixty years ago." Aside from these facts, which present James as an observer of his contemporary world in a way not frequently acknowledged, James's concern with fiction was preeminently a moral concern; he insisted upon the highest degree of cultivation and sophistication in the characters who were the central consciousnesses of his novels. A crisis had therefore to be a personal moral crisis; and the decision taken by his character was therefore not forced upon him but arrived at after a careful and often attenuated moral concern over it. This moral view is international in its nature; it absorbed whatever in several cultures might contribute to its greatest and most heightened receptivity to experience. It is not merely a matter of James's having found a subject or a theme in the international scene; rather, the Italian, the French, the English, the American worked repeatedly in his novels toward a balance of sophisticated and basically ethical sensibilities. Once that balance had been achieved and revealed, he was in his view more eminently capable of discussing and treating social and moral issues; for he felt that they *issued from,* and that their significance *centered upon,* the manner of their having been taken in by the individual conscience.

The point of greatest difference from the naturalists was James's insistence, not arbitrary but perhaps conditioned, upon the nature of that conscience—on the one hand, his sophistication; on the other, his almost invariable social status. There is, after all, a humility (usually called a snobbery) in his feeling that his most vitally relevant characters should have come from the world with which he was most familiar; the point is that James contributed to them not only (and far from primarily) the status of a social class but also an educated and highly perceptive consciousness. They possessed, therefore, a vitality of scruple, to put against the muscular vitality of an uncomprehending McTeague or a vulgar Cowperwood. Their scrupulosity was in one way the consequence of a minute concern over the art, as James had seen it—as a formal development (with such technical results as we have seen) of the moral intelligence surveying its world not "in the large," but, as F. R. Leavis puts it, as "a matter of personal relations between members of a mature and sophisticated Society." So that the question of moral purpose is inextricably bound to the question of aesthetic fitness (and truth in this sense is in direct relation to accuracy of insight and not to breadth or grandeur of social reference). As James has definitively said, ". . . the deepest quality of a work of art will always be the quality of the mind of the producer. In proportion as that intelligence is fine will the novel, the picture, the statue partake of the substance of beauty and truth. To be constituted of such elements is, to my vision, to have purpose enough. No good novel will ever proceed from a superficial mind; that seems to me an axiom which, for the artist in fiction, will cover all the needful moral ground: if the youthful aspirant take it to heart it will illuminate for him many of the mysteries of 'purpose.' "

It follows also that the method used to criticize most adequately such fiction as arises from this point of view will be that of analysis—of the degree to which James's "ideal civilized sensibility" will by inference and subtle revelation of motive provide a deep moral insight dramatically contained. Such an analysis might profitably be used in each of a score of places in James's fiction—as indeed in the fiction of others. It has a devastating effect upon fiction hastily contrived or dependent on other than a literary means. In the case of its most fruitful results, it demonstrates the value of "inflection" and "implication"; as Leavis said, "a nuance may engage a whole complex moral economy and the perceptive response be the index of a major valuation or choice."

iii

The place of James in modern American fiction has not always been fairly judged. James was not a popular novelist; *Daisy Miller* (1883) was his one clear triumph. Except for a few isolated figures, his discussion of his methods—the "story of a story"—did not lead to a serious development in the art of fiction, at least not during his lifetime. Contemporary with him, however, and most certainly of a mind with him in his earnest resolve, Mrs. Edith Wharton perhaps remains the greatest single example of a confiding and sympathetic concern. For all her travels to Europe and her "exile" in France, Mrs. Wharton was more solidly aware than was James of the specific American reality that goes into the making of so much of her fiction. That she had learned much from James's work (perhaps more from his conversations, at which she was frequently present) is abundantly evident in her little book, *The Writing of Fiction*. She remained, not a disciple but an individual artist working with similar matters. *The Reef* (1912) shows her working most closely within the art and method laid down in James's criticism and practice; it is a brilliantly successful novel in the Jamesian mode. But for the most part, Mrs. Wharton had her own field to cultivate. Her greatest affinity with James would seem to lie in their fundamentally similar concern over a precisely formulated moral evaluation of their subjects—moral, as distinguished from social, political, or economic.[2] This involved the clear knowledge of standards; they were standards that Mrs. Wharton understood more clearly than did James—or perhaps it might be said, rather, that she possessed a narrower, a more local view of their context and originating circumstance. As we may infer from her comments on James's techniques, she was also less willing than James to persist in the implications of a technical strategy. The purview of her fiction was most generally a compromise between an omniscience, of which she did not entirely approve, and a tortured submission to the point of view of her creatures. There is a concern over them that may charitably be called maternal or feminine; and there is an obviously but cleverly contrived and manipulated assistance given them in her novels. Perhaps that is because she was not so ambitious for them as James was for his. They do not often achieve the position of "splendid isolation" that the Jamesian consciousness assumes; they are objects more often of pathos—victims rather than interpreters of the circumstance to which they address their attention. This means also that Mrs. Wharton's novels follow more conventionally along the lines of the contemporary "novel of manners." She is given to weaknesses of structure, to a softening of the structural line at points where it needs to be hard and inflexible—as the conclusions of *The House of Mirth* (1905) and *The Age of Innocence* (1920) testify.

The early work of Mrs. Wharton suggests an almost in-

2 Mrs. Wharton did discuss social and economic "issues" in her fiction, but with much less facility and skill than one sees in James's *The Princess Casamassima* and *The Bostonians*. Her *The Fruit of the Tree* (1907) is concerned with economic problems in a New England mill town, though its major dramatic and moral conflict involves the question of a mercy killing, and the whole depends too much upon issues which interfere with careful integration of materials.

flexible concern over a simply devised moral equation: *The Greater Inclination* (1899), *The Touchstone* (1900), and *Sanctuary* (1903) are developments of the theme of temptation and propriety: each clearly defined as is the conflict between them. *Madame de Treymes* (1907), with France for its setting and the international contrast for its theme, takes the Jamesian problem at its bare minimum and treats it with an earnest economy and barrenness of manner. *The Valley of Decision* (1902) is Mrs. Wharton's most active tribute to the George Eliot of *Romola;* like *Ethan Frome* (1911) and *Summer* (1917), it is an exception to Mrs. Wharton's usual themes.

Her principal novels, those published from 1905 to 1920, treat of a setting and a theme which profit from her intimate knowledge and her steadfast concern. The place is New York City and its immediate surroundings, the time chiefly the second half of the nineteenth century. The theme, upon which she rings a number of changes, is the moral decline of an older New York which is under attack by the raw new industrial and financial world. Mrs. Wharton has a clear view of the point from which the decline has begun and has therefore to be judged. I have previously described the world dominated by this view. It was

. . . a world clearly remembered by her because entertained chiefly in memory. Every dollar of it was worth exactly one hundred cents; every act was the end-expression of hard, pure motive; the sensibility of her hypothetical world was uniform and immediate in its perceptions, direct and unquestioning in its adherence to forms. Such a world was made up of streets clearly seen and slowly and gracefully traversed; of names which were traceable to America's beginnings and held to with a gracious persistence as social and moral symbols; of arts limited by her own taste in gardens and furniture; of moral decisions made with the most exquisite sensitivity to the discreetly proper and the most graceful scorn of expediency and compromise. It was a world in which renunciation of the even slightly improper was inevitable and predetermined, moral relaxation a source of horror and the beginning of lifelong atonement.[3]

This was a purified and almost entirely abstract ideal point, to which Mrs. Wharton's novels refer in their detailing of exceptions to it. Responsible for the breakdown of this world were, of course, the post-Civil War industrial and financial maneuverings. These made a clear-sighted judgment, or even a view, of social conduct extremely difficult. With them came a new type of person, whose background had not been so fortunate or so principled. In an important sense, such novels as *The Custom of the Country* (1913) are an exhaustively detailed portrayal of the triumph of the new group over the old. Elmer Moffatt of Apex City is the new financial "barbarian," whose values and incentives are so vigorously opposed to those of the older society that because of sheer strength of will they are able to conquer against negligible resistance. Mrs. Wharton is not without her ironical reserve concerning the ease of conquest. Her "guardian" of the earlier world, Ralph Marvell, has been educated into the very manners that will make him easy to remove; when the precise and honest standards and taste have become mere formulas, they are subjects of ironic commentary rather than of respect:

The only essential was that he [Marvell] should live "like a gentleman"—that is, with a tranquil disdain for mere money-getting, a passive openness to the finer sensations, one or two fixed principles as to the quality of wine, and an archaic probity that had not yet learned to distinguish between private and "business" honour.

3 Hoffman, "Points of Moral Reference: A Comparative Study of Edith Wharton and F. Scott Fitzgerald," in *English Institute Essays, 1949* (New York, Columbia Univ. Press, 1950).

This passage is a more than usually gratifying example of the usefulness of Mrs. Wharton's irony: the phrasing, the inflection, the tone are neatly and cleverly designed to compress characterization and criticism into a small space. "Like a gentleman": the gentleman of Ralph Marvell's world had been held to what was left of originally firm and valid standards. In his time, they had degenerated in such a way as the ensuing phrases ironically describe. The disdain for "mere money-getting" is not vigorously active or morally effective; it is tranquil, which is to say, passive, smugly inactive, escapist. As for the finer sensations, they have long since ceased to be the tasteful accompaniment of a meaningful social life, and Marvell has only to possess a "passive openness" to them. The next phrase suggests to what these finer sensations are now attached. But the passage has a two-edged meaning; the "archaic probity" testifies not only to Marvell's weakness but to the immorality of the new business world as well. The private and the "business" honor had once been one and the same thing; it had been strongly believed that Fifth Avenue should know what Wall Street was doing. Ralph Marvell had therefore "not yet learned" that this older and stricter view of propriety was becoming ineffective. The concluding phrase of this passage has, therefore, a quality of implication which not only her novel but the novels of contemporaries like Howells, Fuller, and Herrick were concerned with expanding and developing. The effectiveness of Mrs. Wharton's novel is due at least in part to her having had in full measure a sharply defined basis of criticism and ironic comment. This criticism is almost mathematically exact in its reference to an earlier society now weakened and almost overcome by the raw, new energy of Apex City's Elmer Moffatts.

Once she had made up her mind to accepting the decline

from the decorum of her world, Mrs. Wharton was able to provide her public with a number of novels which extended the comedy of manners and added to its details. In short, the purpose of both *The House of Mirth* (1905) and *The Age of Innocence* (1920) is to provide a mild and sophisticated comment upon the social comedy of that decline. Her judgment of it, however, is never exclusively derisive or condemnatory. In each case, her hero and heroine have the advantage of a touching reserve of affection and pathos. Lily Bart of *The House of Mirth* is forced because of circumstance to "beg," to live a humiliating parasitic life in a society which is pledged chiefly to finding as many distractions as its resources will permit. In her circumstance, Miss Bart must avail herself of whatever opportunities society will offer. She has been endowed, rather arbitrarily, with a basically strong moral sense, which, on the one hand, prevents her giving in to the inducements of Simon Rosedale (symbol of the aggressive new wealth), and, on the other hand, keeps her conscientiously away from the sanctuary of Lawrence Selden's love. The only other choice is for her to act as companion at the parties and on the Mediterranean excursions of her more fortunate friends. The climactic death of Lily Bart, flirting as it does with the idea of suicide, is Mrs. Wharton's testimony to the endurance of moral integrity. But this is a specious intrusion in a comedy of manners, which, it would seem, is forcibly turned into tragedy. What *The House of Mirth* does contribute, however, is a twofold commentary in support of Mrs. Wharton's theme: both Lily Bart and Lawrence Selden are victims of the social and moral decline of New York society. Both must refuse entirely to give in to it, and are thus defeated by it. Selden withdraws into the chaste and inviolate sanctuary of his library and his sensibility. It is in his library, symbol of the staying power of decorum, that Lily comes to admit her love and to burn incriminating papers as a proof of her invincible integrity.

Throughout, Mrs. Wharton speaks of a world and a history that she knows intimately. The dramatic intensity of her novels recommends them to a comparison with James's most successful manner. The three crucial conversations held by Newland Archer and Ellen Olenska brilliantly and economically sum up the social and moral pressures of *The Age of Innocence;* in this novel, the formulas of New York society have a dramatic meaning that is held in an eminently successful aesthetic control. Archer is himself a man of limited intelligence; he has, therefore, to be reminded on several occasions of the literal significance of the standards of which he has given a rather naïve interpretation. Archer is the articulate, literal embodiment of those standards. He becomes, therefore, the point-of-view character whenever Mrs. Wharton needs to state both the comical and the dramatically serious intent of her social criticism. But it is in the Countess Olenska's soberly literal interpretation of those standards that the pathos of their effects is seen. The points of view in this novel are three: Archer's is supplemented and given its tragic meaning at critical points by the exercise of Ellen's precise and honest moral discretion. Over both of these stands the author's own interpretation. *The Age of Innocence* is an excellent example of Mrs. Wharton's skillful use of point of view: she does not believe in James's splendid intelligence, nor does she wish to retreat as far as James does from the center of the novelist's judgment. Like Willa Cather and especially Ellen Glasgow, Mrs. Wharton wishes to "be there," in a position to offer her own comment upon the fictional circumstance. More than that, she never relinquishes her grasp of the inhibiting details which often make such a creation as a "central intelligence" quite improbable. She knows both Fifth Avenue and Wall Street too well to have created either a Christopher Newman or an Adam Verver.

The dividing line in Mrs. Wharton's achievement is the year 1920, when *The Age of Innocence* was published. Subsequently, she published a great number of novels, but they seem an almost annual testimony to the decline of her powers and to the growing weakness of the formula she had earlier so successfully followed. Some of her work after that year is quite adequate as structure; but the neatness of pattern is only a superficial precision in the working out of a formula already overworked. There are minor felicities in *The Children* (1928); *Twilight Sleep* (1927) must certainly have satisfied abundantly its reader's fondness for the grossly clever social burlesque; and *Hudson River Bracketed* (1929) is a courageous attempt to describe a world to which she was inadequately adjusted. But one has invariably the feeling in these and her other post-1920 efforts that these things are being done more successfully by a generation of writers who know their circumstances more fully and more clearly. The major theme had been exhausted for her in the fiction of the years 1905 to 1920; and in the 1920's and 1930's she either echoed it plaintively or gave in entirely, as in *The Glimpses of the Moon* (1922) and *The Gods Arrive* (1932), to a post-Victorian, *Ladies' Home Journal* slickness of sentiment.

James's influence can, of course, also be seen in the work of Willa Cather and Ellen Glasgow discussed later in Chapter 3. A more conspicuous, if less fortunate, influence is seen in the work of Anne Douglas Sedgwick, who lived abroad from 1882 to her death in 1935. A conspicuous example of her almost slavish attention to Jamesian preoccupations and methods is *The Little French Girl* (1924), which has, among other things, the attenuated rather than subtle development of contrasts, in this case of the French and English temperaments and cultures, as well as a number of James's most frequently used strategies of dialogue and structure. *Tante* (1911), *The Old Countess* (1927), and *Philippa* (1930) also reveal Miss Sedgwick working assiduously with matters of point of view and dramatic dialogue. With Mrs. Wharton, Miss Sedgwick followed the Jamesian manner long after it had ceased being fashionable and before James had (about 1940) regained a position of considerable importance among newer writers. But her talent was a minor one and her indebtedness to James was often too patently her chief claim to the reader's interest and curiosity.

iii

In his brief study of Edith Wharton, Alfred Kazin has usefully pointed up the difference between her view of the growing American industrialism and that of the progressives and muckrakers:

Edith Wharton . . . could hate, and hate hard, but the object of her hatred was the emerging new class of brokers and industrialists, the makers and promoters of the industrial era who were beginning to expropriate and supplant her own class. She disliked them no less fiercely than did the rebellious novelists of the muckrake era—the Robert Herricks, the David Graham Phillipses, the Upton Sinclairs; but where these novelists saw in the brokers and industrialists a new and supreme condition in American society, Edith Wharton seemed to be personally affronted by them. . . . She had no conception of America as a unified and dynamic economy, or even as a single culture. There was old New York, the great house in Lenox (from which she

gazed down upon Ethan Frome), and the sprawling wilderness
that called itself the Middle West, a land of graceless manners,
hoary jests, businessmen, and ridiculous provincial speech.

A major theme in American fiction was not made available to her. Though she knew to a nicety the progressive
stages of New York's financial history, and could therefore
excel James in realistic and convincing portrayal of its moral
and social effects, her understanding of what lay west of
New York was only slightly less hypothetical than his. And
it was probably more erroneous because more dominated
by prejudice than by blissful ignorance. Our concern at
this point, therefore, is with the novels of her contemporaries who dealt with this scene and these facts knowingly
and in a manner quite differently orientated.

A most important and a sadly neglected theme in modern American fiction is that of the gradual withdrawal from
the Jamesian *mise en scène* to the marketplace. The question here is: How can a novelist treat the immediate present
honestly, realistically, and yet retain discretionary powers
over the ultimate judgment of that present? Frank Norris
had somehow encountered that problem in *The Pit* (1903),
in which Curtis Jadwin alternates between drawing room
and trade-exchange; he is a victim not only of the shifting
fortunes of the exchange but of his author's shifting interest
in both polite society and naturalistic forces.

The crucial point in the history of the non-naturalist fiction which deals with this world is William Dean Howells's
conversion to social purpose. The Haymarket riots and the
subsequent executions became for Howells "The thing forever damnable before God and abominable to civilized
men." The importance of this sentiment does not lie in its
having stimulated such novels as *A Traveler from Altruria*

(1894) and *Through the Eye of a Needle* (1907), but rather in its effect in bringing the sensibilities of a novelist highly sympathetic with the art as James saw it to bear upon such matters as James neither acknowledged nor cared to notice in his fiction. In a sense, Howells and James stand at the beginning of a century with talents and interests markedly similar but with quite different uses for the history of our fiction. It was not only Howells's own particular version of realism, which he gives us in *Criticism and Fiction* (1891), with its emphasis upon the commonplace, antiromanticism and democratic literary scruple; nor are his generous tolerances of "the worthy young" and his most fortunate opportunity to help them the sole measure of his importance. Rather, it is in the gradual development of the stand he took with respect to the American economic and social life that he links most significantly to the history of modern American fiction. He was, from experience, training, association, incapable of the raw and formless naturalist disclosures of that life. He could see a Silas Lapham clearly, but not a Frank Cowperwood.

It was natural enough, therefore, that Howells should have written about the mild and temperate matters which engaged the interests of his own class: marriage, middle-class and upper-middle-class manners, travels abroad and the contrasts of manners these invariably disclosed, courtships and marital decisions—even post-marital differences. The delicate issue of such a novel as *The Lady of the Aroostook* (1879), for example, had engaged both Howells's view of what a most proper young American man might discreetly do and his knowledge of American society in Venice. *Indian Summer* (1886), on the other hand, exploited fully both a setting (Europe) and a situation to which Henry James often had recourse. Even here, however, Howells had neither the ambition nor the pretension of assuming any such quite subtle or sustained examination of social and moral choices. As he quite disarmingly admits in a chance dialogue of that novel, his is never quite the "great world" of James's fiction:

"Mr. Colville concealing an inward trepidation under a bold front; Miss Graham agitated but firm; the child as much puzzled as the old woman. I feel that we are a very interesting group— almost dramatic."
"Oh, call us a passage from a modern novel," suggested Colville, "if you're in the romantic mood. One of Mr. James's."
"Don't you think we ought to be rather more of the great world for that? I hardly feel up to Mr. James. I should have said Howells. Only nothing happens in that case!"
"Oh, very well; that's the most comfortable way. If it's only Howells, there's no reason why I shouldn't go with Miss Graham to show her the view of Florence from the cypress grove up yonder."

The strong and deep moral judgment which Howells exercised upon his creatures is no more fully seen than in the portrayal of Bartley Hubbard's decay, in *A Modern Instance* (1881). Hubbard is a major specimen of the way in which that judgment has led to extensions and distortions of characterization in Howells's work. The standard he uses is not that which he subsequently employs in *A Hazard of New Fortunes* (1890) and *The Quality of Mercy* (1892). It is a strictly moral judgment which he calamitously visits upon Hubbard in Tecumseh, Indiana. The avenging angel, Squire Gaylord, proves as disagreeable in his virtue as Hubbard is made unpleasant in his moral weakness. But *A Modern Instance* makes it easy for us to discern the direction Howells was to take in his later, social fiction. Inevitably, Hubbard's untidy morality is linked with dishonest practices in business. Bartley is, in short, untrustworthy and selfish; these are defects of character and personality which eventually ruin the lives of several other characters in the novel. More important for our purposes, translated into the world of business, they threaten the moral structure of the American economy and invite the invasion by kindred spirits of the business world.

The point of the criticism is moral and discretionary; the point of view is that of a highly moral, Christian, liberal intelligence, whose dismay over political and economic inequities is in keeping with his quite proper and quite limited standard. From this beginning, Howells's judgment of business proprieties continues to be so restricted. Progressively we see characters judged "from the outside," as it were, editorially—they are never quite *created* for editorial purposes, but they always suffer a loss of their value and integrity as characters because their author has larger and more external purposes to which they must, he feels, be put.

The prototype of the old-fashioned businessman, the pet of the progressives, is Silas Lapham. His virtue (and it is a very real one, very convincingly given) is that he does not ultimately abandon the "New England standard" of judging his acts and the acts of others. In a business crisis he is capable of acting only on the assumption that private and business honor are the same thing, that his conscience will not permit shady deals, even if they may be legally acceptable. The concluding dialogue is a quite eloquent testimony of Howells's predominating concern over what he regarded as a complex moral crisis in modern business:

"We can trace the operation of evil in the physical world," replied the minister, "but I'm more and more puzzled about it in the moral world. There its course is often so very obscure;

and often it seems to involve, so far as we can see, no penalty whatever. And in your own case, as I understand, you don't admit—you don't feel sure—that you ever actually did wrong this man——"

"Well, no; I don't. That is to say——"

He did not continue, and after a while Sewell said, with that subtle kindness of his, "I should be inclined to think—nothing can be thrown quite away; and it can't be that our sins only weaken us—that your fear of having possibly behaved selfishly toward this man kept you on your guard, and strengthened you when you were brought face to face with a greater"—he was going to say temptation, but he saved Lapham's pride, and said—"emergency."

Howells and the minister both believed in such saving distinctions as that between "temptation" and "emergency"; and in his other novels, he never quite gave them up. They treat of a world that is breaking away from such limited effective moral judgment. But, like his fellow moralists, the Progressives, he could not either attach an unequivocal socialist blame to the new world nor merely document it and explain it in naturalist terms.

In the course of a very few decades, the picture of American expansion made it more and more difficult to explain or to monitor the business world through the use of such a conscience as Lapham's. The heroes of "muckraking novels" were not so fortunate in either their authors or the circumstances of composition. Robert Herrick, whose point of vantage was the academy, did give us the tragedy of the theme—the gradual move toward complete, amoral commercialism, which would eventually all but corrupt the soul of the middle class, dwarf and defeat the earnest will of the Laphams who had survived an earlier history, and render ineffectual the liberal hero of his fiction. He had no confidence in reform; he could not see himself apologizing for a condition by reference to natural forces; he simply accepted the tragedy fatalistically as an irremediable *fait accompli*. Perhaps the only solution that seemed possible under these circumstances was a contrived one—a change of heart or a change of vision, which led decency back to the scene from which it had already been peremptorily dismissed.

What Herrick, Fuller and Phillips gave us was an abundance of detail—in the case of Phillips, the abundance came close to naturalist documentation. The work of all of these men represented the decline of the liberal sensibility—or, rather, its defeat by immediate circumstance, which made such a treatment of it as Howells provided in *The Rise of Silas Lapham* either unlikely or unconvincing. Fuller's *The Cliff-Dwellers* (1893) is a melancholy testimony of their enforced submission to this circumstance; it is a thorough document of the mastery of material over the artist. There were certain inevitable consequences which such a life must have, dislike them as you may; and Fuller all but exulted in his determination to do them full justice.

These novels testify to the decline of the Jamesian moral perception. From Howells through Herrick, we note a tendency to abandon the individual character's control over the shaping of external fact, or at least over its personal meaning—to the point where, in *The Cliff-Dwellers* and other novels, the facts are only in themselves meaningful, and character merely a victim of them. Social realism, in whatever form and for whatever purpose it assumed, had replaced what Lionel Trilling, speaking of James, has called "moral realism." The consequences for the art of fiction were various; they may be said to have followed disastrously the line of diminishing confidence in the individual's capacity for moral decision. *The Rise of Silas Lapham* has in its own way a masterful structure, simply designed in terms of supplementary points of view regarding a central problem. *The Cliff-Dwellers,* Herrick's *Together* (1908), *The Common Lot* (1904), and other novels show that the careful equilibrium of individual conscience with social fact had become increasingly difficult. Social criticism, or "social realism," in American fiction was again taken up in the 1930's, with a number of rather radical changes in point of view and treatment of social document or evidence. Perhaps the most persistent novelist of the early "Progressive" tradition was Upton Sinclair, whose seminaturalist documentaries depended usually upon the immediate pertinence of their materials for their success. Sinclair's work, like that of Herrick and Fuller, continued to appear in the 1920's. Typical of Sinclair's enduring concern over immediate issues are such novels as *Oil!* (1927), which treated the oil scandals of the Harding administration, and *Boston* (1928), concerned with the newly concluded trial and executions of Sacco and Vanzetti.

iv

The twofold contribution of Henry James to modern American fiction can be conveniently summarized. In his preoccupation with method, with point of view, and with the precise integration of every element of a fiction, James gained a moderate following in his lifetime, but mostly censure for what Bennett and Wells, among others, felt was an excessively narrow and prohibitive aesthetic concern with a form that demanded inclusiveness and detail. As a critic of fiction, he has gained enormously in following in recent years; and in various ways, both his critical and his practical interest in form have affected such various talents as

Faulkner, Glenway Wescott,[4] Peter Taylor, and Jean Stafford. What Edith Wharton has had to say about James's own attenuation of basically sound techniques is undoubtedly a valid criticism. Nevertheless, James's sharp insight into the novelist's responsibilities to his art has directly or indirectly served to increase considerably the novelist's awareness of his necessary disciplines; this by way at least of offsetting some of the less fortunate persuasions of naturalist writing in the novel's American history.

As for James's effect upon the treatment of social issues in the novel, it may be said to have begun with his mild objection to Zola's practice and to have been reinforced in his discussion of social and moral didacticism in the novel. It would seem to be a simple enough lesson, but novelists did not stop to learn it carefully or thoroughly. There has been a steady decline of this perception from James's time to ours; and both the novels of the "muckrakers" and those of the leftists of the 1930's have given in to the assumption that external fact and event are overwhelmingly important in fiction. It is only in a few isolated recent novels, like Arthur Koestler's *Darkness at Noon* (1941) and Lionel Trilling's *The Middle of the Journey* (1947), that the assumption has been dissipated and the intelligence of character is shown to act upon event, to modify and make accurate its genuine meaning and importance.

4 Especially in his *Pilgrim Hawk* (1940), a work of great subtlety and technical mastery.

2

PREWAR NATURALISM, 1900–1915

i

THE very label *naturalism* often seems erroneously convincing, and leads critics and literary historians to classify indiscriminately. Some critics apparently feel that, as American fiction proceeded to the mid-century mark, there was a "good" naturalism and a "bad" one: that some novelists had rescued their characters from the naturalist impasse, while others had delighted in meaningless horror. The novelists writing what is roughly called naturalist fiction have contributed to the modern novel an opportunity, or a number of opportunities. They have been largely instrumental in discrediting (perhaps with greater effectiveness than Howells) the falsification of human nature provided in the romances of nineteenth-century and early twentieth-century fiction. They have given a precedent for a documentary style, which, in all its crudity may be utilized in any way an author chooses. They have also encouraged a great democracy of subject—the acceptance of matter which Howells's "Young Girl" could not tastefully allow in the fiction she permitted herself to read; in short they have, in Philip Rahv's words, successfully fought "the long-standing inhibitions against dealing with the underside of life, with those inescapable day-by-day actualities traditionally regarded as too 'sordid' and 'ugly' for inclusion within an aesthetic framework."

Their failure has been chiefly in the matter of symbolic organization and in the difficult task of subtilizing the novelist's conception of event and character. Whatever symbols are used in naturalist fiction strike one as having been arbitrarily chosen and not essentially relevant projections of the material. Once decided upon, they are often repeated with a clumsy insistence. The art of condensation should be a fundamental requisite of the novel. However, naturalists have generally preferred expansion: to add to an event details not needed for a grasp of it does not always lead to sharper insight into it. Finally and primarily, because the naturalists did not or could not often submit to any discipline (or because they sought the wrong disciplines), most of their novels are extraordinarily weak where a novel ought to be genuinely strong—at the crucial point where event, motive, decision have all to be unified in language and structure.

For those writers who, at the turn of the century, provided America with "naturalist fiction," the philosophic

---

1 This "Young Girl" of Howells is used by him as an arbiter of taste in *Criticism and Fiction;* for a full description of her type, see the heroine of his *The Lady of the Aroostook.*

and scientific condition of the late nineteenth century seemed of first and all-consuming importance. Even so, one has always to keep in mind a warning often given, as in this statement by Charles Walcutt: "All naturalistic novels have meanings and effects which are not even implied by the philosophical or scientific theories of naturalism." These meanings and effects are in part the result of the novelist's rejection of, in part the result of his imperfect understanding of, the theories. The novelist's interest in his characters and the assumptions accepted from the theories often run at cross-purposes. Novelists are willing to violate the strict view, if not at will, at least when convenience dictates. It is one thing to accept a world view with all its arbitrary effects and consequences for the description of human nature, quite another to follow through consistently in documenting the fate and fortune of a character within the restrictive limits of a novel. Haphazard popular interest in scientific theories—and the fundamental ignorance underlying the use made of them—plays well into the hands of such a novelist, who finds it possible in one place to postpone, in another to abandon, naturalist conclusions as he proceeds in his work.

Nevertheless, these theories were there, and they were respected, as convenient (and sometimes imperative) explanations of human nature. The philosophic imperative led for one thing to a subordination of character, a withdrawal from immediate and intimate perception, and at the same time to a passive documentation, which imposed upon a character (in the hope of explaining him) an abundance of minutiae. In each separate case, the naturalist view of man and of his relationship with the universe is altered, violated, redirected, in accordance with the formal and aesthetic need of the novel in question. In general, naturalist theory argued for determinism, demonstrable in several ways, with varying emphasis upon heredity and environment as the determinants. Social determinism, or man-made evil, was often given as one explanation. The times in which these novels were written were those of industrial expansion, of endless violations of democratic principle, and of apparently inevitable brutalities committed against humanity. On the one hand, inferences from science (especially those made by Herbert Spencer) seemed to explain and often to condone these conditions. On the other, they were seen as peculiarly American, as a part of the American socio-economic history, hence at least eligible for correction and amelioration, the first and most important step of which was exposure. In some of these records—Crane's *Maggie* (1893), for example—there is a quality of indecision regarding the conditions described; the first inference is that they are inevitable and irremediable; the second, that the characters are in themselves so weak and morally so passive that they deserve what happens to them. The world of *Maggie* is a social wasteland created, not by men who exploit it, but by those who live in it, and who are incapable of living anywhere else. In other novels, the social conditions are described with an implicit (almost never an explicit) criticism of the moral ambiguities which they reveal: the obvious irony of the difference between moral convention and actual social practice.

Finally, a growing list of novels, beginning perhaps with Upton Sinclair's *The Jungle* (1906), was marked by an earnest attempt at *exposé*, with the aim of criticizing either society at large or (by way of effectively localizing the blame) the exploiting class or the parasitic leisure class which availed itself of the fruits of exploitation. This type of fiction, an outgrowth of the nineteenth-century realist novel, maintained a critical bias toward its subject that may be called "Christian" and "liberal." The liberal imagination had insisted upon, in fact, was nourished by, a view of moral progress. It believed that an important step in this progress was a full recognition of social defects, of those conditions which blocked progress toward a utopian state. Since intelligence was required for the recognition and judgment of these defects, the judge in many cases was a liberal intelligence—sometimes a character in the novel, as in many of Robert Herrick's; sometimes the author's voice and mind. The social evil was both immediate and widespread; the intelligence was often burdened by it, even disastrously defeated by it, and became more a pathetic victim than a rational judge.

Most or all of the formal characteristics of naturalistic fiction derive in one way or another from the necessities of theory. "The *document*" was the goal set by the novelist; and the document was designed seriously as proof or objective record. Science and philosophy used the author: in his earnest endeavor to keep abreast of "the latest" that science had to offer, he frequently became (and his art became) a servant of theory rather than a master of it.

For this reason, documentation was regarded quite arbitrarily as a control factor in the arrangement and construction of plot. Not only mere awareness of contemporary or historical issues, but industrious and diligent research into the facts, collation of facts observed, a journalistic zeal in accounting for mass of detail: these were the order of the day. Dreiser, Norris, Crane, and London had all served their time as reporters; the reportorial experience either was the sole formal training or loomed much larger than any other in the discipline of the novelist. The diligently kept-up notebook, the habit of "moving into" an area of observation, assiduous "reading in" or "doing up" a subject—these were regarded as necessary preliminaries for the naturalist literary act. Of all the naturalists, Dreiser was the most industrious, the most literal-minded concerning the store of fact needed for authenticity and conviction, Crane the least. Crane was potentially the greatest artist of them all, gave the most of his imagination to the formal limitations of his subject. Norris was perhaps the most daring, the most educated (in having been exposed to more formal and academic disciplines than the others), and the most exuberant. All these men suffered from a lack of serious formal criticism of the art of fiction.

R. P. Blackmur, speaking of Richard Wright's *Native Son,* says that it is "one of those books in which everything is undertaken with seriousness except the writing." This provocative remark may also be applied to much of the naturalist product at the turn of the century. Certainly the problem of the novel (of the writing and arranging of it) was in each case one to be met and solved as the author could see his way to meeting it. But as for the writing, the novelist and his reader attended to it with negligible seriousness. The audacity, courage and largeness of conception, and its contemporary relevance, both motivated its author and stimulated its reader. Other kinds of success (success of controlled and disciplined writing) seemed, in the light of the total product, to be almost accidental. Even these occasional successes (Crane's *The Red Badge of Courage* and *The Open Boat,* Norris's *McTeague*) were never wholly sound, and were spoiled by post-climactic revisions, additions and concerns. We can say that this writing was honest but that it was frequently not acute, was often gross and inept. The symbolic controls are often introduced suddenly and then held to tenaciously and repetitiously, without any subtlety or genuine relevance.

Preconceptions about society, its problems, its people, are likely to give rise to characterization that is subordinate to an *abstract idea* of character. The naturalist needed to give a character an environment of facts which support him or make him "real"—that is, endow him with the superficial reality one observes from an "El" platform or in the tabloid newspapers. In the criticism of fiction, the question of subtlety and the degree of sharpness of insight into character are important matters. The naturalist writer found it possible to present an illusion of great tension which, when examined closely, is actually achieved only through external action, physical contact—or at best, through loud and strenuous rhetoric. The moments of highest tension are usually those of extreme action, when the mechanics of motion, of physical bodies in conflict with each other or with a grandiosely conceived setting (Nature in its extreme, antarctic forms) are at their peak of obvious performance. Under these circumstances, the reader is almost bound to apprehend, not motive, but body—mass, form, bulk—and is pledged to see action as the demonstration of a preconceived idea.

One of the most skillful portrayals of tension through the description of physical action is to be found in Frank Norris's *McTeague*. The nature of the two characters locked in deadly combat (Trina and McTeague) determines the nature of that tension and of its issue in action; Norris's description requires skillful shifting of vantage point, a reserve and caution of exposition. McTeague has come to the school where Trina works; he is drunk but "alert, unnaturally in-

telligent, vicious, perfectly steady, deadly wicked." Trina,
instantly aware of the crisis, fights back, briefly with words,
then with fists. These two deadly enemies cannot delay action by means of saving dialogue; the dialogue is merely a
sparring before action begins:

> "For the last time, will you give me that money?"
> "No."
> "You won't, huh? You won't give me it? For the last time."
> "No, *no*."

Norris is obviously not interested in the dialogue, except
to restrict it to the limits of his characters' minds. It is not
hastily done; it is simply not done at all, save as a brief exchange between persons whose bodies and not their minds
demonstrate their wills. The flaws in the description of the
action are not serious; they argue occasionally a slight failure of pace.

Beside herself with terror, Trina turned and fought him back;
fought for her miserable life with the exasperation and strength
of a harassed cat; and with such energy and such wild, unnatural
force, that even McTeague for the moment drew back from her.
But her resistance was the one thing to drive him to the top
of his fury. He came back at her again, his eyes drawn to two
fine twinkling points, and his enormous fists, clenched till the
knuckles whitened, raised in the air.

In this brief description of powerful action the tensions
become almost explicitly real; they are far better explained
than are those of many other passages in the same novel, in
which Norris's disposition toward McTeague *as type* forces
him to interfere with the characterization. It is not the action itself in this scene, but rather the restraint in the de-

scription of it that makes the passage so effective.[2] After this brief passage Norris shifts his point of vantage and withdraws from the principals; the cat, hidden behind the coal scuttle, is allowed to hear out the struggle to its conclusion:

In the schoolroom outside, behind the coal scuttle, the cat listened to the sounds of stamping and struggling and the muffled noise of blows, wildly terrified, his eyes bulging like brass knobs. At last the sounds stopped on a sudden; he heard nothing more. Then McTeague came out, closing the door. The cat followed him with distended eyes as he crossed the room and disappeared through the street door.

Crude as this is ("like brass knobs," "distended eyes," "on a sudden"), it approaches a point of almost perfect effectiveness of tone, consistent within the limits of space, character, and action. A mastery of fact (not merely *knowing* fact but possessing skill in seeing it) is one of the best of naturalist attainments. It is fundamentally a realist's skill, involved as it is in a nonsymbolic maneuvering of fact, controlled only by a sense of balance and discretion. But the naturalist's extension of this skill, or his use of it, often involves its subordination to an ideational purpose, almost always amateurish, at best imperfectly understood. It leads to what are all but unpardonable errors of judgment—to forced, ideologically determined coincidences and parallels through which the "world view" is expressed. It leads also to crude symbols, to out-of-character dialogue and gestures, which are remote from any simple realization of realistic truth. McTeague and Fleming suffer less from this fault of maneuvering than

---

2 It should be noted, however, that this is an isolated skill—a skill that it is good to have, of course, but one that is not a major characteristic of great fiction. The same skill can be seen eminently if only temporarily effective in such slick novels as John O'Hara's *Appointment in Samarra* (1934), where the total effect is gross rather than serious and more likely to titillate the senses than to challenge the intelligence.

do most characters in naturalist fiction. It is, in fact, of a piece with the unfortunate consequence of the "scientific view" which Henry James so shrewdly discerns as one of Zola's obsessive concerns:

Science accepts surely *all* our consciousness of life; even, rather, the latter closes maternally round it—so that, becoming thus a force within us, not a force outside, it exists, it illuminates only as we apply it. We do emphatically apply it in art. But Zola would apparently hold that it much more applies us.

ii

There were matters in American naturalist fiction not to be found (at least not in their local quality) in the fiction of French antecedents and contemporaries. In addition to the particular social and critical direction which naturalism took in America, the fictional applications of theory were abundantly modified by other considerations. One of these was the perdurable interest in "the great American novel." Indeed, the American continent seemed so vast and so various that it both challenged and defeated efforts to encompass it, or to get to its heart or essence. This was national color, as opposed to local color, though novels of this kind often sought for the ideally suitable region from which a discussion of the American "essence" might come.

In such novels, contrary impulses often obscured naturalistic purpose. One of these was a native brand of mysticism, or the manufacture of a myth, "made in U.S.A." The historical incentive was provided in the wishful pantheism of Whitman's poetry and prose. The desire was understandable, the results curious and interesting. Its contrarieties are best seen in the naïve and unwittingly ironic structure of Frank Norris's *The Octopus* (1901). The contradictions in the mind of Norris' point-of-view character, Presley, are his own too:

Just what he wanted, Presley hardly knew. On one hand, it was his ambition to portray life as he saw it—directly, frankly, and through no medium of personality or temperament. But, on the other hand, as well, he wished to see everything through a rose-coloured mist—a mist that dulled all harsh outlines, all crude and violent colours.

Norris himself wanted more than that: he wanted occasionally to find and state a metaphysical cause. He wished also to provide an almost Howellsian moral drama, in the discussion of Magnus Derrick's struggle to choose between propriety and political effectiveness. He gave all of these; in addition, he provided, in what he called "the big, epic, dramatic thing," Dickensian portraits and Breughel-like scenes. The execution of this varied purpose could not help leading to contradictions: moral judgment at times harsh and intolerant, at other times soft and irritatingly gracious; coincidences of event and parallels of action which gave rise to a cheap and mechanical irony; above all an unevenness of pace that could only have been the result of a fundamental conflict between Norris's descriptive and activist strategies.

The ambition which motivated the American "epic" was closely related to the more abstractly vague of naturalist incentives. Naturalist generalizations had presumably to be large—at once inclusive and universally applicable. Since a novel must deal with the specific, the naturalist novel could accommodate itself to that requirement only by multiplying instances, by assimilating and accumulating details, and sometimes by becoming broad in its scope—in short, by being populated.

Another important American variation upon the naturalist theme was the portrayal of the man of force and violence, the "superman" of the West coast or the Arctic wastes or the sea (or, in the case of Norris's *Moran of The Lady Letty,* a superwoman), to whom is added the super-tycoon of Dreiser's Cowperwood novels. The reasons for this development are partly formalistic and partly melodramatic. In its most abstract form, the physical energy of the universe could be called a "force"; for such novelists as Norris and London that force was brute force or animal instinct. Given the most melancholy of naturalist premises—that man is victim rather than master of his fate—the super-hero entered American fiction as the servant of a melodramatic strategy. The force of the hero should at least match the force which defeats him, and the defeat should therefore be commensurate in energy if not in tragic dignity with the mechanics of the dominating force.

This is only a variant of naturalist practice. Crane's Maggie knows and expresses no such heroism; Dreiser's Clyde Griffiths knows it not; nor do the heroes of latter-day social naturalism, whose actions are governed by the hero-denying theses of unity and co-operation among the proletariat. A strong man or a superman is in this case no Zarathustra—abnegation, contemptuous asceticism, largeness of spirit are not for him; instead, he chiefly possesses muscular strength and animal passion. Both are available for immediate use and upon slight stimulus. In accordance with such greatness, the setting involved is vast and terrifying: the open sea, the floes of arctic icelands, vast stretches of mountain and desert. Even Norris's McTeague cannot be contained entirely within San Francisco streets; his climactic struggle, suitably supported by villainous coincidence, must take place in Death Valley, so that "brute force" may be a match for "natural force."

In an essay published in the San Francisco magazine, *The Wave,* Norris offers another, a less philosophic, reason for this naturalist melodrama. The commonplace, says Norris, is an inadequate means of expressing the human tragedy (he must certainly have rejected the decline of Dreiser's Hurstwood, which is the commonplace made effective by scrupulous repetition). The character of "a naturalistic tale" must possess a violent and energetic greatness; and this greatness cannot be contained within the walls of ordinary circumstance:

Terrible things must happen to the characters of the naturalistic tale. They must be twisted from the ordinary, wrenched from the quiet, uneventful round of everyday life and flung into the throes of a vast and terrible drama that works itself out in unleashed passions, in blood and in sudden death. The world of M. Zola is a world of big things. The enormous, the formidable, the terrible, is what counts; no teacup tragedies here.

Norris asks for considerable desperate maneuvering of character, action, and setting. In the case of Jack London, there is a superman type, the Wolf Larsen of American fiction, who moves in and out of boys' adventure stories, where he properly belongs. The most strenuous examples of these naturalist heroics are to be found in the anticlimactic to-the-death struggle between McTeague and Marcus Schouler, in *McTeague,* several scenes in *Moran of The Lady Letty,* and much of London's *The Sea-Wolf* (1904). All of this is an interesting sideshow in the naturalist carnival, except that in the cases of both London and Norris it argued over and over against the interest of other naturalists in a kind

of proletarian induction. It disappeared from serious literature, to be revived later in another form of the novel of
violence, the novel (ranging from the detective thriller to
the farcical tragedies of Caldwell) in which violence becomes an externalized demonstration of contemporary economic and moral dislocation.

iii

Theodore Dreiser is an ideal test case in the history of
naturalist fiction. His best life story, *A Book about Myself*
(1922), reads like a continuation of his novels—*is*, in large
part, the material of his novels. The early life, in Indiana,
suggests the preparation in Dreiser's experience for the
great "discovery" which he is alleged to have made through
the reading of nineteenth-century philosophy and science.
Religion and conventional ethics were disproved over and
over by the evidence of daily violations. The sinner pros-
pered, the deeply and narrowly religious man suffered. Sincere dedication seemed always to lead to poverty and dep-
rivation. A forced asceticism simply stimulated the desire
for things it denied to him. In these circumstances, Dreiser
was led to a simple equation: desire was fundamentally and
primarily for material things; degree of desire (or "social
stratification") applied simply to the growing need of finer
things, more highly gratifying and more expensive experiences: silks and satins instead of gingham. A further assumption, certainly abundantly documented by Dreiser's
newspaper experience, was that there was no discernible or
measurable balance between "good" and "success"; not the
good, but the strong succeeded. In Pittsburgh, Dreiser tells
us, he first came to the work of Tyndall, Huxley, and

Spencer. Then occurred the electrifying realization: what he had seen of life was not just evidence of a temporary and remediable defect in American society, but the proof of a universal law which neutralized and forever canceled out the effectiveness of any man-made law and convention.

One year at the University of Indiana was the extent of Dreiser's higher education. As for the rest, his training was acquired in newspaper offices; in Saint Louis an editor showed him the MS of a Zolaesque novel; subsequently he read Balzac. From newspaper offices and from his own experience in having to attend to them, he acquired a wholesome respect for facts. The art of telling a story seemed to him to require a marshalling of facts in an order most obvious and most easily followed. His novels thus acquired the rough form that facts naturally achieve when they recur often enough to indicate simple patterns of chronology and repetition.

Dreiser was historically in a position to profit most from these interests and this devotion. His early life, because of its poverty, encouraged his rejection of what he called "moralists" and "religionists"; his rejection met a sympathetic response, especially after his books had been subjected to the conventional shock-reactions of Mr. John Sumner. Facts as such—the more of them, the more effective—were an antidote to the "slop, silly slop" of contemporary romancers. "At least," as one critic wrote, "he was not facile, conventional, superficial, thoughtlessly optimistic." Certainly he was not "thoughtlessly optimistic." More than that, the facts were *fresh,* and Dreiser was overcome by the wonder of them all. He possessed the same rawness of insight and abundance of enthusiasm which had attended the Midwest's naïve "thinkers" of *Poetry* magazine in the 1910's; he had the same satisfaction as they in announcing village profundities as great truths ("The past is a bucket of ashes"; "I am the grass; I cover all"), and the same fresh sense of awe over the sound of words, the surprise that one could actually write them and say them.

Sister Carrie (1900), had, then, the advantage of a fresh, new, arresting event. Its rawness shocked the wife of the publisher whom Frank Norris had prevailed upon to accept the manuscript. For the liberal critic, the muckraker and the tilter at Philistine windmills, *Sister Carrie* was an event of high importance, an importance which has survived sober revaluations of the book. Dreiser gained his hearing at a time when his apologists were anxious to find just such a writer. His followers did not leave him, but increased their admiration with each successive book.

Carrie Meeber discovers that there are three points of view concerning the mechanics of satisfying desire. In the grim semipoverty of her sister's home, she is told that it is best to do without things; the conventions sanction a dreary and monotonous lower-class life. The important step away from that life is at first urged by the drummer, Drouet. Things are within her grasp, if she will take them and accept the marginal morality that taking them requires; she is able to take a further step, to go away with the glamorous Hurstwood and settle with him in New York. Throughout Carrie is a simple, pure soul, touchingly concerned over moral irregularities and becomingly surprised when she discovers the tricks Hurstwood has played on her. Finally, she advances beyond her dependence upon men, when she discovers that her man is not dependable. Carrie's rise marks a quite definitely qualitative change from her earlier life. She becomes self-supporting and is able to afford the kind of life she has dreamed of during the Chicago days. More than that, she achieves financial independence because of her talent as an actress, and there are degrees of excellence there too.

Toward the end of the novel, Dreiser moves toward an "argument," a simple classification of desires as material and ideal. Through the stimulus of the wholesome remarks of one Robert Ames, the third and last man in her life, she is crudely enabled to make distinctions: "the ideal" is more important than things, for one; culture and "the arts" are in the end more gratifying than vulgar wealth; there is more value in being a dramatic actress than in starring in musical shows. The pattern of the last third of the novel seems therefore to have a vague moral purpose. Hurstwood's decline and fall, detailed with the grim exhaustiveness of which Dreiser is master, is concurrent with Carrie's rise. At the end Hurstwood is dead, and Carrie is unhappy. Nevertheless, there is no overt preaching in the description of Hurstwood's decay. Instead, there are amateur chemistry and physiology. Dreiser's moral interpretations are given in pseudoscientific terms. Above all, the novel urges us to accept these two characters as passive, and on the whole, as will-less, creatures. Hurstwood suffers, not punishment for a crime, but the debilitating effects of a change in environment plus the compounding evil of a slowing of energy. In New York he has none of the material support for the self-confidence of his Chicago days. Discomfort and poverty serve to increase the difficulty of making another start. Potter's field is the end result. Its cause is cumulative; we are held fascinated by the growing pattern of disenchantment and dissolution. In the end, we have an exhaustively documented anatomy of misery. Throughout the novel, we sense something of the fresh, naïve, uncynical wonder of the setting in which the narrative proceeds.

In the interval between the first publication of *Sister*

Carrie and the publication of his next novel, *Jennie Ger-hardt* (1911), Dreiser supported himself in various ways, chiefly as editor of *The Delineator,* a woman's fashion magazine published by Butterick. *Jennie Gerhardt* celebrates another woman, gives us still another portrait of the weakness of the male and again deals with illicit love and other unconventional matters. Jennie, like Carrie, is victimized by poverty. She suffers further misfortune when the distinguished father of her illegitimate child inconsiderately dies before his promise of marriage can be fulfilled. Jennie has the strength of the uneducated but faithful Dreiser woman. Social stratification prevents her from marrying Lester Kane, son of a wealthy manufacturer. In time, Kane uncomfortably realizes Jennie's limitations, and he marries a woman of his own class. But Jennie triumphs in the end; Kane gives her his deathbed assurance that she has always been the only "true love." The social implications of the novel are similar to those of *Sister Carrie,* though here Dreiser makes his first attempt to provide some clarity of outline. His purpose here is a variant of that in *An American Tragedy* (1925). Human desires and social conventions are incompatible. A natural and therefore suitable satisfaction of those desires should certainly have been achieved in the marriage of Jennie and Kane. But this cannot happen because of class differences. Jennie, however, has the strength that the hero of *An American Tragedy* lacks. She accepts, is solaced by her feeling of self-sacrifice and by her spiritual resources. Her victory over circumstances (which nominally defeat her) is a triumph of the strongly passive soul. She has none of the discomfort that bothers Carrie Meeber when she hears "the call of the ideal"; nor is she disturbed by the conflict of renunciation with desire which leads to Clyde Griffiths' death. There is little enough of the "brooding inference" in this novel. Like Jennie, we accept the circumstantial defeat, and we are satisfied that there is a power that endures beyond it. With a heavy hand but a tender concern, Dreiser has produced a heroine quietly equal to the stresses and strains of her environment.

Two of the three Cowperwood novels appeared next: *The Financier* in 1912, *The Titan* in 1914. In these novels we discover what at least appears to be a new approach to society and wealth. Cowperwood is an expression of natural forces in America's industrial world, as London's Wolf Larsen is in the purely physical world. He is the "strong man" of the history of American fortunes. There is little or no real criticism in the muckraking manner here; instead, we have Dreiser's wondering, naïve eye, surveying the world of American power politics, the ruthless building of fortunes. He does not criticize Cowperwood; he does not make socialist inferences out of his hero's behavior; he is not distressed (as was his contemporary, Robert Herrick) over the surface moral contradictions of American capitalism. These things exist, they are strong and powerful; and a nicely discriminating moral sense would really be out of place in viewing them. Carrie Meeber had stepped beyond the conventions almost accidentally; Cowperwood shrewdly removes himself from their limits and establishes an ethic beyond conventional good and evil. In doing so, he formulates his own morality of the strong, and sweeps aside all of the niceties of social and political distinction which bother the heroes of James's and Howells's novels. Cowperwood is never concerned over the nicely put and humbly solved moral problem posed for Howells's Silas Lapham; his strength and power enable him to reach beyond any of the restrictions given by Howells to his characters. For Dreiser's Cowperwood, such moral or social censure as occasionally occurs is not much more than an annoyance. In the world of late nineteenth-century finance success seems to have come only to the man of invincible will. The fittest who survive are successful because they are not disturbed by scruple.

The strength of the novel is once again the strength of abundant, unrestrained, and unselected detail. Dreiser's research energy succeeds in providing more than enough of documented fact. In *The Financier* this detail serves fairly well to keep the narrative within bounds. Cowperwood's experiences are fresh and new; his struggles to rise, his efforts to meet early disappointments and to maneuver his way back from defeat all seem credible and mildly interesting. Once he has moved to Chicago (in *The Titan*) and has reached the top level of the financial world, the freshness wears off, and the interest in his activities becomes journalistic. Cowperwood simply repeats himself, in his financial maneuvers, in his purchase of the finer things, in his loves. His extramarital affairs are as drearily monotonous and as witless as are those ascribed to Eugene Witla in *The "Genius"* (1915). Nowhere is Dreiser more inept and fumbling than in his recitals of Cowperwood's and Witla's loves. The women offer themselves without grace or discretion; they have neither the independently searching spirit of Carrie nor the strong will-toward-acceptance of Jennie. They have, in short, only what Dreiser, blinded by his admiration of the dominating male, has left to give them. The fumbling move on his part toward a naturalistic explanation of the chemistry of passion and the natural history of motive has here led to a gracelessness that is almost unequalled in modern American fiction. Dreiser's hero must surely have been as bored with the staleness of repetition as the reader inevitably becomes with this recital of tasteless amours. Dreiser does of course intend an irony in the affair which concludes the second novel, and continues in the third, *The Stoic* (1947); the beautiful and sensitive Berenice Fleming is the daughter of a former "madame"; she is of course innocent of her mother's past. It is with her that Cowperwood withdraws from the Chicago inferno to Europe for spiritual relaxation.

With both *Sister Carrie* and *The "Genius"* Dreiser achieved an American *succès de scandale;* in the latter case, he enlisted the aid of America's imp-of-goodwill, H. L. Mencken. Much of Dreiser's reputation came from its having absorbed an advantage from the crusade against John S. Sumner and Comstockery. Mencken's acuteness was always blunted in a "good fight" for bad literature if it in any way shocked bourgeois sensibilities. But with the publication of *An American Tragedy* (1925), Dreiser made his only genuine bid for critical acceptance aside from such extraneous matters. This novel is the crucial test of Dreiser's excellence, the final challenge to those who would insist that the defects of his manner vitiate its merits.

Despite its great length *An American Tragedy* is simply constructed. Its three parts might be labeled "Description of Cause," "Act," and "Reconsideration of Cause." More than in any other of his novels, Dreiser here took advantage of what may be called a "crucial scene." Beginning there, he determined to explore exhaustively the reasons for it; what circumstances, environmental and psychological, should have led to the death of Roberta Alden? How should that death be interpreted, socially, legalistically, morally? The most painstaking of the explanations is the social, which takes up all of the first part of the novel. Clyde, like other Dreiser heroes and heroines, is a victim of a world in which he is unfortunately placed. His mother and father, street evangelists, teach a religious sanction for poverty which is more than mildly distasteful to him. Crime consists of a series of accidents which follow from simple attempts to satisfy inhibited desires. In addition to being poor, Clyde is starved morally. He is not capable of more than the crudest discriminations, and the hotel rooms which he serves as bellhop do not provide him with any education in moral distinctions. Clyde's experiences thus reinforce his dislike for his parents' preachments. On the other hand, everything newly real and vital for him seems beyond his reach. He cannot be both conventional and morally proper. He is convinced of the impropriety of proper behavior, but he is also physically weak; he is not a strong, brave man, but a moral coward. His instinct is to flee, so long as flight is possible. Society, says Dreiser, stimulates desires which convention makes it difficult to satisfy. Clyde is born poor, and for the poor there is no hope except through one or another kind of amoral stratagem. But a man must be strong if he should hope to violate convention in order to live according to the American standard. He must make and exploit his own opportunities; he must ruthlessly disregard any principle that interferes. Clyde is not capable of ruthlessness; he is a conscientious weakling.

What all of this is supposed to prove, Dreiser does not say; the burden of inference is in favor of social criticism, as the leftists have correctly insisted. The way out for Clyde is found when he meets his uncle, who owns a factory in Lycurgus, New York. He is taken into the factory, first as a common laborer, then as a department foreman. On the level of Clyde's own social origin and background there are drudgery, poverty, and secret meetings with Roberta Alden, a fellow worker. Too late for comfort, Clyde meets his relatives and is accepted in their society. His affair with

Miss Alden has already secured his doom, when he decides that he has a chance for a more gracious and a more brilliant life. The pathetic Miss Alden is a most pitiful victim of both levels of Clyde's opportunity: as the object of Clyde's sexual interest, she becomes pregnant; as the poor but faithful daughter of poor but righteously indignant parents, she is unacceptable in the society of the Griffiths and the Finchleys.

After several half-attempts to solve what on these terms is not solvable, Clyde arranges a trip to a lake, where Roberta is drowned. He does not kill her; the death is accidental. But Clyde is morally responsible for her death—or he is at least convinced that he has killed her before he goes to his death in the chair.

All of this—every detail of it—is exhaustively and grimly reviewed before a jury of Roberta Alden's friends and countrymen in the trial scenes. Belknap and Jephson, in the face of invincible odds, argue for Clyde's moral cowardice; he did not commit a crime, they say, because his courage failed him and because he was inherently incapable of such courage to begin with. He is not morally culpable because he is morally weak. The argument does not succeed; it has no chance of success, in the face of political conditions and local prejudices.

Finally, in the long dreary stretches of time between imprisonment and execution, Dreiser revives the issue of religion in a way quite unusual for him. Clyde's mother is brought from the streets of Denver to New York, where she displays a singular devotion and tenacity of purpose. The character of the Reverend Duncan McMillan is introduced: an earnest, self-sacrificing, persistent cleric, who wears down Clyde's moral resistance to the point of open confession and almost to the point of secret admission of guilt. Religion is not attractively presented here, but Dreiser has come a far way from his earlier amateurish dismissal of it as "Bunk!"

An American Tragedy is a naturalist *tour de force*. It succeeds in spite of its lumbering sprawling self. The method is saturation by overemphasis and detail, rather than enlightenment through selection and discrimination. There is nothing that quite escapes being crude in this novel; the more "refined" its setting, the cruder its achievement. As the novel proceeds the character of Clyde gains in everything but depth: scarcely anywhere in fiction do we know so many facts about a character, or know them from such frequent repetition. But Clyde neither has nor deserves dimension. He is what Dreiser, then Belknap and Jephson, then McMillan, say he is. He has no feeling or insight that is not borrowed. He is the creature of an indefatigable and an earnestly exhaustive omniscience. The crudities of language (not quite so offensive here as in earlier Dreiser novels) argue insistently a fundamental crudity of mind, which is quite unable either to create an inner subtlety of character or to resolve the contradictions of inference which occur throughout as the reader plods steadily through this mass of slowly accumulating fact.

3

WILLA CATHER AND
ELLEN GLASGOW

i

As AN undergraduate at the University of Nebraska (1891–95), later in Pittsburgh as a dramatic critic and editor, Willa Cather found the fiction of Henry James and Edith Wharton exciting and exemplary. "For me," she said, "[James] was the perfect writer." Writing some nineteen years after the publication of her first novel, *Alexander's Bridge* (1912), Miss Cather described the circumstances under which that novel had been written:

The "novel of the soil" had not then come into fashion in this country. The drawing-room was considered the proper setting for a novel, and the only characters worth reading about were smart people or clever people. "O. Henry" had made the short story go into the world of the cheap boarding-house and the shop-girl and the truck-driver. But Henry James and Mrs. Wharton were our most interesting novelists, and most of the younger writers followed their manner, without having their qualifications.

Whatever her backgrounds, Miss Cather had in the earliest years of her career determined to find the best models and to follow them. The hunger for art and for the life of the mind which she must have felt in her life on the prairies served to increase and to encourage her belief in "the best style" and "the highest art." Later she was to condemn the results of this early effort. The writing of *Alexander's Bridge,* she said, "was like riding in a park, with someone not altogether congenial, to whom you had to be talking all the time." This discomfort is often revealed in the style of the novel; she seems anxious to imitate the most stiffly formal of manners:

"Mr. Alexander! I am delighted. Have you been in London long?"

Bartley bowed, somewhat laboriously, over her hand. "Long enough to have seen you more than once. How fine it all is!"

She laughed as if she were pleased. "I'm glad you think so. I like it. Won't you join us here?"

"Miss Burgoyne was just telling us about a donkey-boy she had in Galway last summer," Sir Harry Towne explained as the circle closed up again. Lord Westmere stroked his long white moustache with his bloodless hand and looked at Alexander blankly. Hilda was a good story-teller. She was sitting on the edge of her chair, as if she had alighted there for a moment only. Her primrose satin gown seemed like a soft sheath for her slender, supple figure, and its delicate colour suited her white Irish skin and brown hair. Whatever she wore, people felt the charm of her active, girlish body with its slender hips and quick, eager shoulders. . . .

This is the language of an apprentice writer, self-consciously concerned over the right phrase, the correct dramatic balance, the best precision of setting. The novel is itself a testimony of Miss Cather's mixed emotions regarding her art. She was describing a world she had acquired, to which she had painstakingly and devotedly orientated herself. Henry James had seemed indispensable to her in Lincoln, Nebraska ("In those days, no one seemed so wonderful . . ."); and, as she moved East, she determined to find the ideal setting for the art of fiction, as she believed James had understood it. Through the friendship and advice of Sarah Orne Jewett, however, she was to recognize the value of the world she had left behind. Miss Jewett's *The Country of the Pointed Firs* (1896) had held beautifully within the limits of a region and yet had possessed what Miss Cather called "the perfection that endures."

Miss Jewett wrote of the people who grew out of the soil and the life of the country near her heart, not about exceptional individuals at war with their environment. This was not a creed with her, but an instinctive preference.

On the prairies she had been urged by her reading of James to the perfecting of a sophisticated art. In the East, in the "salon" of Mrs. James Fields at 148 Charles Street, she had been urged by Miss Jewett to "return to the soil." Both urgings seemed to have had a lasting influence; in each case, she was to retain some effects and to add to them her own. The truth was that Miss Cather's prairie (and the principle to which it contributed) was like neither James's London nor Miss Jewett's New England. It made demands on her that the experience of her two principal mentors had not encountered. From James Miss Cather seemed to get her interest in structure, in the use of a point-of-view character, such as Jim Burden, in *My Ántonia,* and in the perfection of sophisticated dialogue. From Miss Jewett, she took chiefly the encouragement she found in her regional successes—the "beautiful writing" which she saw as a consequence of Miss Jewett's steady concentration upon a thoroughly understood scene:

On the coast of Maine [Miss Jewett had written in *Deephaven,* a passage that Miss Cather especially admired], where many green islands and salt inlets fringe the deep-cut shore line; where balsam firs and bayberry bushes send their fragrance far seaward, and song-sparrows sing all day, and the tide runs plashing in and out among the weedy ledges; where cowbells tinkle on the hills, and herons stand in the shady coves—on the lonely coast of Maine stood a small gray house facing the morning light. . . .

In the language of this passage, Miss Cather found nothing that could exactly be transported to Nebraska; the lights and shadows of her descriptions were both more elaborate and less precious. The essential difference lay in the scope of descriptive imagination required in each case. But she was encouraged to feel that she could make her own experience significant, could make literature from it, from the example set. Miss Cather's Nebraska led to a kind of fiction entirely beyond Miss Jewett's scope; both in variety of effects and perceptible range of impression, the novels of Nebraska outdistance the limited views of Maine. The immensity of prairie settings dwarfed the inhabitants and challenged them to an unequal struggle for survival. When Miss Cather turned, therefore, to those settings, in the first of her novels which dealt exclusively with them—*O, Pioneers!* (1913), she found herself far removed from all but the example set by Sarah Orne Jewett:

The little town behind them had vanished as if it had never been, had fallen behind the swell of the prairie, and the stern frozen country received them into its bosom. The homesteads were few and far apart; here and there a windmill gaunt against the sky, a sod house crouching in a hollow. But the great fact was the land itself, which seemed to overwhelm the little beginnings of human society that struggled in its sombre wastes. . . .

ii

The great novels of the prairie states are *O, Pioneers!* and *My Ántonia* (1918). In these novels, with one emphasis or another, Miss Cather had worked out what she thought were the principal themes that literature might discover in that setting. The first of these was the hardness of the land, which offered its pioneering settlers disappointment and disaster more often than success. It was under these conditions that the challenge to character was most severe, and only the strongest succeeded. Strength for Miss Cather seemed, at least in these novels, to be almost solely the possession of women; these heroines—Alexandra Bergson of *O, Pioneers!* and Ántonia Shimerda of *My Ántonia*—are, in the words of T. K. Whipple, "simple, primeval, robust with a strain of hardness, heroic." They must possess a power which enables them to outstay temporary disappointments, to accept the harshness of nature on its own terms and to fight it by enduring it. They must have the faith in the land which comes from identifying oneself with it:

[Alexandra] had felt as if her heart were hiding down there, somewhere, with the quail and the plover and all the little wild things that crooned or buzzed in the sun. Under the long shaggy ridges, she felt the future stirring.

In these novels, the masculine and feminine principles are reversed. It is the heroine who endures, the man who provides the meaning of her struggle and who interprets its results. The men of Miss Cather's novels are the sensitive souls, artists often, out of place and out of sympathy with the rigorous demands of the land. Ántonia's father, Carl Linstrum, Emil Bergson, the young men and artists of several of her short stories—these seem to offer a sensitive view of life that the country cannot accept because it is insufficiently civilized to allow for it. In one way or another, they surrender to circumstance or are victims of it. It is through the women that their loathing for the land, or dissatisfaction with it, is absorbed and dissipated. The triumph over the land is due to the endurance of the heroine; but it is through the male's self-defeating sensibility that other values, alien to the land, are preserved. The simple strength and beauty of such a character as Ántonia Shimerda could not have been appreciated, were it not that her story was told by Jim Burden, who is led throughout and finally to admit the value of the land because of his admiration and love for her. For the same reason, Burden's love for Ántonia cannot lead to marriage; it is fitting that she should marry a commonplace man, who serves her through his almost dumb feeling for the land and its needs. Both Burden and Carl Linstrum leave the prairies for the cities; the responsibility of keeping the land alive and habitable is left to the women. And it is significant that Linstrum should return to marry Alexandra only after her purpose has been successfully fulfilled. Through these means Miss Cather has pointed out the complementary roles of man and woman in her Nebraska novels.

Throughout these novels there is a second theme—the suggestion that the creative artist is in closest sympathy with what Miss Cather regards as the complete life. As she had pointed out the failure of the pioneer community to understand (or to need) the artist, so later she was to suggest that the life of the small towns rejected both the feminine strength and the masculine sensitivity of the pioneer life. Miss Cather's "defeated souls" were from the beginning artists—singers, violinists, sculptors—who, in one way or another, had to get away from the prairies before their art could be nourished and who were appreciated even then by only a few isolated rebels against the dead-level convention of the towns they had left. In one sense, her strongest and most bitter criticism of the prairie culture was that it could not understand or abide the artistic soul. The most fully developed of these aesthetic misfits is Thea Kronberg of *The Song of the Lark*. Her talent might have languished for lack of opportunity, were it not for a handful of eccentric townspeople (all of them men) who encourage it and insist upon it: "Professor" Wunsch, who teaches her what he knows; Dr. Howard Archie, who sees in her talent all that he has missed in life; and Ray Kennedy, a railroad worker, whose insurance money gives her the start she needs in her career. Throughout this novel, the two major concerns of Miss Cather's early fiction are joined. Thea Kronberg must get away—the necessary training and society are not available in this eastern Colorado town; nor are the sympathy and understanding there, which will support her conviction. But the sophisticated East (Chicago, New York, Europe) will never, she feels, take the place of, nor will triumph make her forget, the genuine, self-sacrificing friendship of those select few who have encouraged her to begin.

These themes are in an important sense an indication of the feeling Miss Cather had throughout her life toward her adopted prairie country. She was aware of its great emotional appeal and tragically conscious of its limitations. She would accept it in its earliest form and exult in the opportunity to present its epic struggle toward definition. But the second generation—first described in the figures of Lon and Oscar Bergson of *O, Pioneers!*—had already lost that charm. The next stage of Miss Cather's fiction involved a detailed explanation of her rejection of the modern world. Her first treatment of that theme concerns the small town that grew up on the margins of the great farm settlements. Here there is neither primitive strength nor civilization; there are only smugness and contentment with second-rate feelings and experience. Respectability and a commercial shrewdness were not to her taste; and Miss Cather's share in the "Revolt from the Village" theme in American fiction is to underscore over and over again her dislike of that small, petty, self-contained world. This feeling was to be aggravated, was to expand into a general repudiation of the modern world. The life of the cities displeased her as did the life in these drab towns. *One of Ours* (1922) is a revealing and symptomatic novel. Claude Wheeler's hatred of his father's modern practices is a major expression of Miss Cather's indictment of modernity:

The farmer raised and took to market things with an intrinsic value; wheat and corn as good as could be grown anywhere in the world, hogs and cattle that were the best of their kind. In return he got manufactured articles of poor quality; showy furniture that went to pieces, carpets and draperies that faded, clothes that made a handsome man look like a clown. Most of his money was paid out for machinery,—and that, too, went to pieces. A steam thrasher didn't last long; a horse outlived three automobiles.

Claude's father leaves the farm, to become a salesman of this machinery. Claude himself, like one or two of Mrs.

Wharton's heroes, finds a meaning and a purpose in World War I, where he goes to his death. It would seem also that Miss Cather had rejected the world of Bayliss Wheeler; in her preface to the essays, *Not Under Forty* (1936), she said, by way of explaining its title:

The world broke in two in 1922 or thereabouts, and the persons and prejudices recalled in these sketches slid back into yesterday's seven thousand years. . . . It is for the backward, and by one of their number, that these sketches were written.

A further explanation of her attitude toward the modern world is contained in *The Professor's House* (1925), in the figure and the attitude of Professor St. Peter. The professor's new house is crowded with all of the furniture of modern life that she claims must be thrown out—"stuffy with new things," as she tells us in her preface to the novel: "American proprieties, clothes, furs, petty ambitions, quivering jealousies—until one got rather stifled." In the old house, from which the professor will not be moved, he recalls the story of a favorite student, Tom Outland, whose invention, incidentally, has been exploited by the modern spirit of the professor's in-laws. "Tom Outland's Story" is the story of the return to a primitive world, purified of all of the physical and moral clutter of the modern. The ancient cliff city on the solid, hard mesa offers a security and a refuge for the professor which his author was soon thereafter to embrace.

iii

Death Comes for the Archbishop (1927) and *Shadows on the Rock* (1931) represent not only a shift of interest and concern; they are also examples of a new form. Or, rather, they are a further extension of the manner she had assumed from the beginning:

What I always want to do is to make the writing count for less and less and the people for more. I am trying to cut out all analysis, observation, description, even the picture-making quality, in order to make things and people tell their own story simply by juxtaposition, without any persuasion or explanation on my part. . . . Mere cleverness must go. I'd like the writing to be so lost in the object that it doesn't exist for the reader.

The writing exists—sparse, dry, and reserved, "objective" —in these two novels, but the narrative has all but disappeared. The effect is static and quiet. The formal lessons she had learned earlier from James are here not consciously applied. The spirit is what matters. She is satisfied that here, in the Southwest of the 1850's and in Canada of the early 1700's, she has found a refuge from the clutter of the professor's new house. She is less a conscious artist than a conscientious recorder of the simple lives and faith of primitive peoples. For her these people have retained what the modern world has thrown out. She will have no sympathy with those who—like Hemingway and Fitzgerald—write a fiction about that world; she must withdraw from it. The results are undoubtedly remarkable; her people absorb a simple quality from their environment, from its nature and its hazards, which even her prairie heroines had failed to have. The characters are purified to the point of static, two-dimensional goodness. Their lives have the meaning, and their deaths as well, which a religion literally accepted and believed in confers upon them. They apparently need no refinement which ceremonial and religious art cannot provide. As for the sophistication that Miss Cather had earlier insisted upon, it is still there, but it is only for those who are in a position to use it; it is a sophistication purified of its earlier urban setting, and it is qualified by her insistence upon the greater value of rough souls in a primitive setting.

Some of the sections of these novels contain brilliant writing; Miss Cather's art is nowhere so self-contained. But one has inevitably the feeling that she has given up too much for what she now feels she must have. The purchase price is great indeed. The loss is chiefly in dramatic intensity and in subtlety of representation. The world of these two novels seems a child's world. There are no problems here that cannot be solved by recourse to a simple, abiding faith in a father image. The historical theme which her other novels had tried to give has here been abandoned. However crudely stated, the study of a growing complexity and of a deepening evil in the change from pioneer life to a complex modern life had been vitally given in her earlier novels. Something much more successful might, for example, have been done with Jim Burden's insight and point of view, in *My Ántonia;* or the contrast of *The Professor's House* between the simple and the complex might have been exploited more fully and more skillfully. When Miss Cather returned from Quebec, it was to the prairie states that she decided to go. The portrait of Neighbor Rosicky in *Obscure Destinies* (1932) possessed none of the vigor of *O, Pioneers!,* none of her earlier sense of the climactic struggle of earth with man, but instead settled for a pleasant sentimentality and the warm glow of simple affection. When, in 1935, she tried to revive the theme of *The Song of the Lark* in *Lucy Gayheart,* she had gained some understanding of the towns she had arbitrarily dismissed earlier; but the romance is itself not more than mildly effective. In *Sapphira and the Slave Girl* (1940), she tried for the first time to take up subject-matter closest to the place of her origins (Virginia). Nowhere is her failure as a formal artist more poignantly obvious than in this novel. The characters move self-consciously in accordance with the "great theme" their author must now discuss. The handling of that theme is narrow and inconsequential; and, of course, the shifting of point of view in the Epilogue—in which Miss Cather herself becomes a narrator—is painfully embarrassing.

In an anxious attempt to underscore Miss Cather's significance for the modern American novel, N. Elizabeth Monroe has said that she is one of those novelists "who win a place in public regard in part through the essential nobility of their character and their clear-sighted rectitude rather than through the direct processes of art." This is not quite like saying, as Farrell says of Dreiser, that a novelist can be important for *what* he says regardless of *how* he says it. Miss Cather has, after all, always had a strong sense of the aesthetic requirements of her fiction; this is a conviction for which she was admired not only by reviewers but primarily by fellow-artists. "In a period so marked by devotional estheticism in writing," says Alfred Kazin, "and one when it was easy to slip into the ornamental fancywork of men like Cabell and Hergesheimer, Willa Cather and Ellen Glasgow stood out as examples of serious craftsmanship; and it is strange how easy it has always been to forget how much more brilliant a stylist Ellen Glasgow is than most of the younger writers, and how much more deeply imaginative an artist Willa Cather proved than Hemingway."

That she was deeply aware of the need for the novel to be a formal work of imaginative art, her own essays and prefaces reveal. She had a wholesome respect for the work of James, Wharton, and Flaubert; and she knew where the

naturalists had failed. Nevertheless, there are certain inhibiting weaknesses in the point of view she painstakingly
brought to her art. She was right when she took Sarah Orne
Jewett's advice to write about what she knew best. But we
can only say that her effort to bring to that subject the point
of view of the sophisticated Easterner did somehow fail. It
was not that the techniques recommended to her in her early
apprenticeship were not suited to the Midwestern subject;
they are suited to any subject at all. Rather, she had acquired
a taste and a cultivation as well; and this taste first led her
into an imperfect integration of sensibility with subject,
then finally forced her into a distorted view of the subject
altogether; to the point that, "in 1922 or thereabouts" the
world "broke in two," and her subject did as well. She
found in the plains states a kind of meaningful order—a life
in which acts were closely associated with moral and emotional sanctions. It was not the specious order sentimentally
and falsely lamented in *A Lost Lady* (1923), but an order
she was able to see instinctively in the lives of those people
she best knew. But somewhere in her first years as a writer
she had naïvely accepted the drawing room and the salon as
perfect and distinct refuges of taste; and this view led her to
reject, with embarrassing simplicity of mind, the feeling for
her subject, the attitude toward it that might have given it
the mark of true greatness. On the one hand, she was unable
to reproduce the real vitality of her subject—such as, for
example, Ole Rölvaag was able to give it in *Giants in the
Earth* (1927). On the other hand, she was able to see in the
history of her people nothing but a steady decline and disintegration into cheap materialism. She also failed, therefore, to explore the facts of modernism with the uninhibited
honesty of a Hemingway. And she was left with the role of
chronicler of a simpler society—a society which antedated

her distress with the modern world and thus enabled her to avoid that world.

Miss Cather was a traditionalist who, having acquired cultivation, used it to reject the subject that lay at hand. Most of the younger writers, she said in 1931, followed the manner of Henry James and Edith Wharton, "without having their qualifications." She had herself made the mistake of assuming that the manner of James had somehow also to be rigorously associated with the social setting in which he had developed it. So the manner did her no more than incidental good, and her insistence upon that setting, upon the narrow view of "taste" that dominates so much of her attitude even unto the posthumous *Old Beauty and Other Tales* (1948), damaged immeasurably the opportunity her experience had given her.

iv

Like Miss Cather, Ellen Glasgow is a traditionalist; like her fellow Virginian, she tried to present a fictional account of a region. Unlike her, however, Miss Glasgow stayed with her Virginia, or at the most followed her Virginians into New York City. Her many novels are a solid and concentrated record of the South's history, and of its manners, from before the Civil War to her own times. "While American fiction entertained itself with an historical pageant," she says in *A Certain Measure* (1943), "I began a history of manners that would embrace those aspects of Southern life with which I was acquainted." She divides her fiction into three groups: the historical novels include *The Battle Ground* (1902), *The Deliverance* (1904), *The Voice of the People* (1900), *The Romance of a Plain Man* (1909), *Virginia* (1913), and *Life and Gabriella* (1916). Second is the "country group," which includes three novels concerned with the Virginian countryside and its people: *The Miller of the Old Church* (1911), *Barren Ground* (1925), and *Vein of Iron* (1935). Finally, there are the novels of the city: *The Sheltered Life* (1932), *The Romantic Comedians* (1926), *They Stooped to Folly* (1929), and *In This Our Life* (1941). The novels of the first group constitute a panoramic record of Virginian life, beginning, in *The Battle Ground,* with a portrait of Southern plantation life as early as 1850, and ending, in *Virginia* and *Life and Gabriella,* with a sardonic review of the pathetic remnants of social tradition in modern Virginia. *The Battle Ground* is the most conventional of these novels. Herein are contained portraits of two Virginia plantation families, with all of the attention to the love of learning and good wine, the problem of inherited "bad blood," the strong and faithful heroine, the good and bad slaveholder, the sharp clash of views among friends concerning the slave issue and secession. All differences are resolved in the war's heroic challenge. And the first of Miss Glasgow's engaging heroines, Betty Ambler, gives an earnest of the South's patient resolve to recover and rebuild its fortunes: "the spirit," as Miss Glasgow puts it, "that fought with gallantry and gaiety, and that in defeat remained undefeated." *The Battle Ground* is not without criticism of that tradition. There is more than a suggestion here of what Miss Glasgow later more fully realized:

In the old South, this inherited culture possessed grace and beauty and the inspiration of gaiety. Yet it was shallow-rooted at best, since, for all its charm and its good will, the way of living depended, not upon its own creative strength, but upon the enforced servitude of an alien race. Not the fortunes of war, not the moral order of the universe, but economic necessity doomed the South to defeat. In the coming industrial conquest, the aristocratic tradition could survive only as an archaic memorial. It was condemned to stand alone because it had been forsaken by time.

Here, briefly, was a theme (or a succession of themes) richer in body and in possibilities than that available to Willa Cather, richer even than the substance of the social history to which Edith Wharton had attended. As a novelist of the South's economic and political history, Miss Glasgow is interesting and passionately concerned; but it is in her quiet management of the social comedy of manners that she gives of her best insight and writes in her best manner. There is, above all, the pathos of the beautiful woman who is born out of her time (Virginia Pendleton, Eva Birdsong), whose grace and beauty are wasted upon the remnant of an earlier "grand society." There is also sharp criticism of the cultural attitudes which, for all their candlelight charm, serve more to hamper than to enhance the heroine's career. Virginia "was more than a woman," writes Miss Glasgow; "she was the embodiment of a forsaken ideal." Having been educated to the requirements of the ideal, she found herself the victim of a world in which "even man, who had created her out of his own desire, had grown a trifle weary of the dream-images he had made." The "code of beautiful behaviour" had its other victims as well. There are, for example, the pathetic spinsters who pay the penalty of a "fatal" indiscretion or of an unattractive appearance. So, Aunt Agatha of *They Stooped to Folly,* Cousin Etta of *The Sheltered Life.*

Miss Glasgow remarks that "In my own critical opinion, my best books have been written since 1922 . . ." During this period she wrote the so-called comedies of manners which remain, along with *Barren Ground* and *Vein of Iron,* her best-known works. It is well, therefore, to determine in what lies their excellence. They are heavily weighted with their author's own brand of irony; they have their own kind of moral commentary upon the South's disparate fate; they are, furthermore, exercises in formal composition. The irony is itself of a kind most easily available to an author who had lived through decades of its almost daily reminders. Men and women who have survived a tradition and yet adhere to its code always manage to call attention to that sad history. Moreover, the tradition is itself threadbare, sometimes a little cruel, often patently ridiculous.

With what is often not more than a grudging recognition, Miss Glasgow acknowledges the presence of the modern man and woman, who, like John Welch of *The Sheltered Life,* impatiently dismisses the faded grace of the tradition. More often, as in the case of General Archbald of the same novel, she regrets the passing of what must seem to her a strong social code vitiated by selfishness and cheap commercialism. Like Mrs. Wharton's latter-day aristocrats, these people of Miss Glasgow can only regret what is happening to them; they cannot prevent it, nor can they prevent the active disasters which its own weaknesses have caused. The point of view of the old Civil War General of *The Sheltered Life,* deeply embedded as it is in his past, provides us with the full pathos of her ironic theme. Archbald, who had himself been a rebel against the more virile aspects of the tradition (he could not stand the sight of blood and was therefore of no value on hunting trips; he had helped in the escape of a Negro slave), in 1917 looks helplessly upon the tragedy of its effects. The modern reincarnation of the tradition is George Birdsong. Charming, irresistibly attractive to women, he inspires the "grand love" and then is incapable of remaining faithful to it. He is symptomatically fond of hunting; his great annual experience is the fall session of duck hunting. In the dramatic last scene, the twenty-five ducks he has brought back from his last ceremonial excursion serve as ritual symbols, also serving Miss Glasgow's irony and pathos well—the more so because they are viewed both with the sense of immediate horror and with the retrospective chagrin of the old man. This exercise in point of view which Miss Glasgow has permitted herself here gets the very best from the sacrifice of the ducks who are ritual victims, as the Birdsongs are neurotic victims, of a defeated tradition.

There is, of course, more than that. Both the Archbalds and the Birdsongs have remained in a district of Queenborough (Richmond) that had at one time been the fashionable home of the city's most favored society. The devastating effects of progress invade their doors, penetrate to their very nostrils. There is a bad smell from the factory district nearby which, if the wind is right, makes life unbearable. The smell is the most vivid reminder of the New South's triumph over the Old. The only weapon against it is Mrs. Archbald's "idealism"; she can pretend it away, or so her father-in-law insists. Nevertheless, it is hard to maintain one's grace and charm in such an annoying circumstance. That the tradition should have been so reduced by its own weakness that a factory stench is the reminder of its decay serves as Miss Glasgow's culminating ironic commentary upon it.

For all its pervasive and telling presence, Miss Glasgow's irony is often an inconvenience. She was, after all, a conscious and careful artist. As early as *The Deliverance,* she was concerned with the problem of measuring the range of point of view in her characters. She had in that novel religiously concerned herself with the narrative consciousness of her hero, Christopher Blake. This was a conscientious dedication to a principle advocated by Henry James. The structural planning of her novels in terms of point-of-view characters had been, she said, an instinct with her: "Instinct alone had warned me that a narrative should adhere to the central figure, and that looseness of structure, as well as thinning substance, was the result of a too variable field of vision." Her ingenuity in handling point of view is demonstrated often in her novels: *The Sheltered Life* begins with the vision of the young girl, Jenny Blair, who is "going on ten"; the second section gives us the point of view of General Archbald's "deep past," painfully returning to the present a few times. The final long section combines the two points of view so that the tragedy of the Birdsongs might be seen from the tortured and agonized vision of both the very young and the very old. *The Romantic Comedians* seldom leaves the point of view of the elderly Judge Gamaliel Bland Honeywell. All that happens in the novel is either a judgment by him or a judgment of his belated romantic decision. *They Stooped to Folly* distributes the narrative responsibility fairly equally between Virginius Curle Littlepage and his wife Victoria. The other characters (Milly Burden, Marmaduke, Mary Victoria, Mrs. Dalrymple, Aunt Agatha) are in one way or another subject to the modes of regret, firmness, doubt, or exasperation consequent to the views each of the principals has of the tradition. The pattern thus imposed on the novel is at once intricate and complex. For the most part *In This Our Life* is narrated with the consciousness of the defeated Asa Timberlake either fully in use or actively in mind. *Vein of Iron* applies again the technique employed in *The Sheltered Life:* except for the early chapters, the points of view are two, the young girl, Ada, and her father, John Fincastle. "The eyes of youth," Miss Glasgow explains, "must look on life through the cour-

age of emotion, while the eyes of age regarded it through
that fortitude which wisdom bestows."

This maneuvering of point of view is one of the most
interesting facts of Miss Glasgow's art. The difficulties it
encounters are not so much the consequence of the method
itself, which, as her intuition had told her, was sound. It is
primarily because she was quite unable and unwilling to
give her point of view characters a free hand, or their consciousnesses free reign, that the method often fails. Especially in *The Romantic Comedians* and *They Stooped to
Folly*, the author's witty omniscience invades the consciousness of her narrating character and by that much makes him
less effective in his chosen role. What readers so much admired in the first of these novels was actually not the Judge's
rationalizing and fumbling mind but Miss Glasgow's sharp
and witty commentary upon it.

"I am a bird with a broken wing," he sighed to himself, as he
had sighed so often into other ears since the day of his bereave-
ment. And while this classic metaphor was still on his lips, he
felt an odd palpitation within the suave Virginian depths of
his being, where his broken wing was helplessly trying to flut-
ter. *(The Romantic Comedians)*

Did she really care for him, he wondered, oppressed by the responsibility, or was she obeying some general law of the woman's
impulse to cling? What illogical memories women possessed!
What disastrous loyalties! True, he craved the lost flavour of
youth; true, he longed, in safe places, for the perilous fires of
romance. But he knew now, beyond any doubt, that the only
romance he needed was the kind that did not give serious trouble. Prudent rather than possessive, he kissed her clinging lips,
and turned quickly away. *(They Stooped to Folly)*

There is more of omniscient control and interpretation
in these and many other passages than of a careful use of

the point of view decided upon. Miss Glasgow is here and elsewhere not really exploiting the point of view so much as she is maneuvering her characters into the position of puppet-voice. The damage done is most fully seen in *They Stooped to Folly,* where the complications never become more than a product of reiterated interpretive comment upon a theme which the characters are scarcely ever able to individualize. Too often, they are obliged to speak in generalities that are only tangential to their personal, emotional share in their meaning. And their minds seem (conspicuously, in *In This Our Life*) to share monotonously in a trite sentiment of unresolved and scarcely articulated feeling.

v

For all her animadversions on a dying tradition and its ridiculous or pathetic remnant, Miss Glasgow, in common with Willa Cather and Elizabeth Madox Roberts, had also to assert the value of a more primitive, and therefore more enduring heroism. In a sense, the two novels most prominent in this mode *(Barren Ground* and *Vein of Iron)* are a kind of revenge for the sins committed by the tradition with respect to its womanhood. "For once, in Southern fiction," Miss Glasgow says in *A Certain Measure,* "the betrayed woman would become the victor instead of the victim." More than that, she was to represent "a dynamic force," triumphing not only over her betrayer but over the whole decline and enfeeblement of the land and its people. Like Miss Cather's Nebraska heroines, Dorinda Oakley and Ada Fincastle possess the knowledge and power that ride out all adversity and make strength where weakness threatens. Dorinda "would never lose her inner fidelity, that vital affirmation of life, 'I think, I feel, I am.' The only thing that mattered was her triumph over circumstances." Where mere man had faltered, Dorinda passionately succeeds. In *Vein of Iron* the woman has the strong assistance of her father, whose fortitude and will are reinforced by his learning, his devotion to scholarship and to his special kind of idealistic metaphysics. But even here the pattern established in Willa Cather's Nebraska novels is maintained, except that the enduring racial strain is early and old American and not that of recent immigrants. The necessity to affirm would seem urgent in the face of what must be called the melancholy conclusions of her novels of the city. The city can form a setting for an ironic comedy of manners or a symbolic tragedy of the death of tradition; but it is from the country, from the lives of the people on the land, that the conquering affirmation must come. Hence it is that the city scenes of *Vein of Iron* add up to a valiant but vain struggle against the depression-evil of the spirit; and the death journey of old John Fincastle back to his country home points the way to the renewal and cleansing of the spirit suggested in the novel's concluding chapter.

As Miss Glasgow, in her novels of manners, has imposed herself upon her characters and themes, never trusting them to an independent development, so here she affirms beyond the permission of her materials. There is no reason to doubt that such affirmative spirits as her heroines could have existed, but they are presented too often as "affirming beyond their means," as being too passionately and too personally implicated in what are, essentially, rhetorical generalizations. One feels that this is less true of Dorinda Oakley than of Ada. But it is curious to see that, in her first novel, *The Time of Man* (1926), Elizabeth Madox Roberts, working with what is a comparable subject, should have remained free of rhetorical exaltation and enforced affirmation. The behavior of Ellen Chesser, in that novel, seems always quietly to correspond to the feeling and the assertion of which she is capable. The pleasures and the discomforts of farm life in Kentucky, the vagrancy of her men folk, the endurance required to survive poverty and violence—these are all there, but there is no attempt to make of them anything that is not accurately to be inferred from the novel's details. What there is of poetry in the novel is defensible in terms of the folklore and folk-song of the people themselves.[1] There is too much contrived pathos in *Vein of Iron,* especially in the chapters which treat of Queenborough during the depression years. And though Dorinda Oakley is more convincingly given, we are forced too often to see her as a model of heroic womanhood: "She exists wherever a human being has learned to live without joy, wherever the spirit of fortitude has triumphed over the sense of futility."

Ellen Glasgow thus imposes both an all-embracing ironic commentary and an urgent sense of affirmation upon her materials. In the former case, we are frequently prevented from seeing them seriously enough; in the latter, we are told that we cannot think too seriously of them. A truthful and in the end a more effective handling of them would not have forced us into either predicament. Unlike Miss Cather, whose artistic concern resulted mainly in a retreat from her subject, Miss Glasgow is too much with hers. Pruning and arranging, grouping and ungrouping, always anxiously directing our attitudes toward it, she too often defeats her

1 Although *The Time of Man* is Miss Roberts's only genuine success in the treatment of her native Kentucky region, it is only one of several novels she published: among the others were *My Heart and My Flesh* (1927) again treating of the poor tenant farmers of Kentucky and accurately transcribing their speech; *The Great Meadow* (1930), a novel of pioneer life in Kentucky; and *He Sent Forth a Raven* (1935), in which a mystical love and fear of the land gets in the way of an honest use of the materials she had so excellently managed in her first novel.

most conscientiously attended purpose. She has a much firmer grasp of the structural needs of the novel than does Miss Cather; nowhere in her fiction is there quite so dismal a failure to grasp them as in the latter's *Sapphira and the Slave Girl*. The defects of Miss Glasgow's fiction are in a sense a consequence of her often acknowledged advantage. She knows her materials from a constant repetition of them; the attitudes, the ironies, the pathos that they inevitably suggest tend through ceaseless iteration to lead to stereotyped work. Too often the meaning they deserve to have through the natural, clear inference available to every reader of a successful novel is not delayed beyond the initial pages. For all her skill in formulating the social epigram, the half-witticism—one might almost say because of it—the dominating intelligence of her fiction lies on its surface; it is not often seen working closely or effectively within the materials themselves. With the same kind of intelligence, Mrs. Wharton was able, in her occasional successes, to achieve a much sounder and a more valid work—a fact that needs for its confirmation only a routine comparison of the crucial passages of *The Age of Innocence* with, say, those of *The Romantic Comedians*.

4

GERTRUDE STEIN: THE
METHOD AND THE SUBJECT

i

IN 1903, Gertrude Stein settled in France, the earliest of the twentieth-century expatriates. *The Autobiography of Alice B. Toklas* (1933) is Miss Stein's record of the first thirty years of that life and of the impression it made on a number of admiring young Americans who found their way to 27, rue de Fleurus. "Gertrude Stein never corrects any detail of anybody's writing," she says in that book; "she sticks strictly to general principles, the way of seeing what the writer chooses to see, and the relation between that vision and the way it gets down." Unlike Ezra Pound, who was in Paris from 1920 to 1924, and Ford Madox Ford, the editor of the *Transatlantic Review* (1924 and 1925), she influenced through the art of conversation and advice, not by means of the blue pencil. Her advice was received with great respect. "Ezra was right half the time," Hemingway is reported to have said, "and when he was wrong, he was so wrong you were never in doubt about it. Gertrude was always right."

Hemingway provides a good case study of Miss Stein's influence upon the writing of his generation. Speaking of one early manuscript he had submitted to her, "There is a great deal of description in this, she said, and not particularly good description. Begin over and concentrate." He was a "good pupil," she insisted against the objections of Miss Toklas, and Sherwood Anderson supported her: "You don't understand, they both said, it is so flattering to have a pupil who does it without understanding it." He was eager to learn, devoted to the discipline of writing, and came away from her talks chastened and inspired. Copying a part of the long manuscript of *The Making of Americans* (1925) for publication in Ford's *Transatlantic Review*, and correcting the proofs, he "learned a great deal and admired all that he learned." Arguing at one time with her about the worth of Anderson's writing, he heard some remarks on American literature which have since become a part of modern criticism:

Gertrude Stein contended that Sherwood Anderson had a genius for using a sentence to convey a direct emotion, this was in the great american tradition, and that really except Sherwood there was no one in America who could write a clear and passionate sentence. Hemingway did not believe this, he did not like Sherwood's taste. Taste had nothing to do with sentences, contended Gertrude Stein. She also added that Fitzgerald was the only one of the younger writers who wrote naturally in sentences.

The purpose of all this conversation and of Ezra Pound's thorough criticism of the manuscripts, was to achieve precision of statement, to avoid what Hemingway was later to condemn as faking. The margin of difference between faking and honesty in writing was often a narrow one, but it took into account chiefly the source of the writing: if it had been taken over from the reading of other people's work, it was almost sure to be less than accurate or true; if it came only from what Miss Stein called "remembering," that is, from experience not one's own, it was not clear or true; it must have come directly from experiencing and must therefore have a sense of immediacy. Many adjectives were likely to indicate an attempt to impress which falsified the report; abstractions (unless they were useful) were an example of faking; images had to be controlled, or they would, like adjectives, lead away from the subject. The aim was concentration, and this aim led to a major emphasis upon the sentence, as opposed to large plans and tricks, even to the paragraph itself. It was the individual sentence that she admired in Anderson's writings—as for the paragraph, he had a very vague notion concerning the logical requirements and importance of such a unit of composition. On one occasion, watching her dog Basket drink water, Miss Stein said "that listening to the rhythm of his water drinking made her recognise the difference between sentences and paragraphs, that paragraphs are emotional and that sentences are not."

ii

In the course of her writing and lecturing, Gertrude Stein developed a thorough explanation of her work and a definition of what she called composition. She was of the opinion that a generation needed to attend to its own experiences, which were always different from the experiences of other generations. A writer can do only what "is seen" and in the way that it is seen: "The only thing that is different from one time to another is what is seen and what is seen depends upon how everybody is doing everything," and "Nothing changes from generation to generation except the thing seen and that makes a composition." These remarks, from her Cambridge lecture, "Composition as Explanation," perform for modern prose what Pound and T. E. Hulme had done for modern poetry. She was interested in preventing dull, empty repetition of thoughts not related to "the thing seen" and in underscoring the importance of the available experience for writing, which must be different from "the thing remembered," with a difference basic to the preservation of accuracy in the art of prose.

The composition is the thing seen by everyone living in the living they are doing, they are the composing of the composition that at the time they are living is the composition of the time in which they are living.

Perhaps nothing that she said in this lecture was not already implicitly recognized in her first book, *Three Lives* (written in 1905 and published in 1909). Especially in the second of these Lives, "Melanctha," is the careful and intimate working out of her theory of composition evident. Of this theory there are three principal divisions: that of "beginning again and again," which has to do directly with the style of writing; that of maintaining a "continuous present," or what she also calls a "prolonged present"; and that of "using everything." The first of these is actually a means of achieving the second and involves the third. It involves also the consequences for style of constant iteration, an almost ceaseless turning back to, or upon, a subject, a thought, often in the manner of a simple mind trying to make clear what he is thinking. As a consequence, Miss Stein felt, the slight shades of difference that exist in all things that superficially seem identical may be brought out:

It was all so nearly alike it must be different and it is different, it is natural that if everything is used and there is a continuous present and a beginning again and again if it is all so alike it must be simply different and everything simply different was the natural way of creating it then.

The significance of this criticism for modern writing is that it never abandons its insistence upon the thing seen, or felt, or experienced. This thing is the starting point, and not merely an incidental detail, of the writing; from there, we may have "a series" and the series of things seen may eventually prove to have a logic of development and narration, a "structure" which comes from its being a series. But even "when there is a series," Miss Stein insisted, "Beginning again and again is a natural thing. . . ." And it is a dangerous thing to forget the varied nature of the "discrete instant," or to abandon it, or to impose upon it large "notions" or ideas to which it is negligibly related, if at all.

Some of the characteristics of modern prose have a direct bearing upon this explanation. [Miss Stein was more interested in the isolated sentence, in its rhythm and its succession of meanings for the thing it is describing. She could have little to do with the problems of structure; nor could she go beyond a certain point in her influence upon modern fiction. In fact, for some writers—noticeably, Sherwood Anderson—who did not possess sufficiently a sense of compositional strategy or whose view of character was limited, her influence could only make them repeat awkwardly what they had earlier done more effectively. Like the cautionary discipline of imagism in poetry, Miss Stein's explanation and practice could make an excellent but a limited contribution to modern writing; it could point to an indispensable minimum of the art, but there remained other disciplines of mind and imagination which depended upon an individual writer's capacity for developing.

Given the control and discipline necessary for the development of a novel beyond the mere practice of beginning again and again, it is nevertheless true that the writer who had listened to her (even though, as she said of Hemingway, he "does it without understanding it") often secured his work against faults of composition, perception, and insight. The writing would be true to the thing seen or thought, so true as to see all of it and so true as to see nothing that was not there. Examples of Miss Stein's prose which illustrate this principle of integrity and the effectiveness which is its result are abundant, though perhaps the "Melanctha" section of *Three Lives* will serve best:

Jeff Campbell never knew very well these days what it was that was going on inside him. All he knew was, he was uneasy now always to be with Melanctha. All he knew was, that he was always uneasy when he was with Melanctha, not the way he used to be from just not being very understanding, but now, because he never could be honest with her, because he was now always feeling her strong suffering, in her, because he knew now he was having a straight, good feeling with her, but she went so fast, and he was so slow to her: Jeff knew his right feeling never got a chance to show itself as strong, to her.

Although it is true that the style of this is relatively conventional (that is, there is a minimum of the "beginning again and again") and there is more of the active movement from one stage to another of narrative "progress," the passage serves to illustrate several of the characteristics of her prose which attracted her followers. There is nothing that does not genuinely belong to the subject—no decorative imagery, no attempt to break through the mind and feeling of the Negro whose mind it explores, to impose upon him auctorial orderings of his thought, no imagery of any kind. This is not to say that Miss Stein did not allow her writing to be colorful when its subject itself was colorful, but simply that here the subject demands and gets honest treatment —that is, treatment limited to its nature. This is all the more obvious and impressive when the whole of the tortured relationship of Jeff Campbell and Melanctha Herbert is put before us, as it is in *Three Lives*.

Passages from the fiction of Hemingway's generation illustrate the importance of Gertrude Stein's advice and practice: this one, for example, from Hemingway's *A Farewell to Arms* (1929):

I had gone to no place where the roads were frozen and hard as iron, where it was clear cold and dry and the snow was dry and powdery and hare-tracks in the snow and the peasants took off their hats and called you Lord and there was good hunting. I had gone to no such place but to the smoke of cafés and nights when the room whirled and you needed to look at the wall to make it stop, nights in bed, drunk, when you knew that that was all there was, and the strange excitement of waking and not knowing who it was with you, and the world all unreal in the dark and so exciting that you must resume again unknowing and not caring in the night, sure that this was all and all and all and not caring.

Or this passage in Anderson's "I Want to Know Why," from *The Triumph of the Egg* (1921), an insight into a young boy's mind which has in it echoes of Mark Twain's *Huckleberry Finn* as well:

Sunstreak is different. He is a stallion and nervous and belongs on the biggest farm we've got in our country, the Van Riddle

place that belongs to Mr. Van Riddle of New York. Sunstreak
is like a girl you think about sometimes but never see. He is hard
all over and lovely too. When you look at his head you want to
kiss him. He is trained by Jerry Tillford who knows me and has
been good to me lots of times, lets me walk into a horse's stall
to look at him close and other things. There isn't anything as
sweet as that horse. He stands at the post quiet and not letting
on, but he is just burning up inside. Then when the barrier goes
up he is off like his name, Sunstreak. It makes you ache to see
him. It hurts you. He just lays down and runs like a bird dog.
There can't anything I ever see run like him except Middlestride
when he gets untracked and stretches himself.

iii

The fiction of the postwar years derived from a number
of other places, of course. Besides Gertrude Stein, there
were Ezra Pound and Ford Madox Ford in Paris. Pound
was chiefly interested in poetry and hoped only that good
poetry might be written as well as good prose. He had wished
to transfer some of the qualities of good prose to poetry, and
he was especially interested in what he admired in Ford's
novels—*The Good Soldier* (1915), for example, and the
Tietjens series of war novels.

Ford's indefatigable work as an editor of the manuscripts
of young unknowns has been abundantly described for us
in Douglas Goldring's books, *South Lodge* (1943) and
Trained for Genius (1949). As editor in chief of the *Transatlantic Review* he came in closest association with the
young American expatriates. They seemed all to be from
the Midwest and to want to turn their attention to that section of America, as he tells us in his introduction to *Transatlantic Stories* (1926).

Ford was interested in problems of the novel that went
beyond the limits of Gertrude Stein's concern. Through

him the most important matters of point of view and structure in the novel which had concerned Henry James and Joseph Conrad were translated into the discourse of postwar writing. The experiment of the "qualified first-person" narrator which he had successfully tried in *The Good Soldier* had an effect upon F. Scott Fitzgerald which can be seen in his use of Nick Carraway in *The Great Gatsby* (1925). Above all, there was his security of taste with respect to the language itself. He feared the trickery of the English language and respected the virtues of simplicity with a wholesomeness that won the respect of the Young America that had moved from the limitless prairies into Paris after World War I. He was, moreover, the advance agent for Conrad's works, pushing forward the recognition of his novels so they were read seriously, for their very marked values of form and technique. Like James before him, and Pound in his own time, Ford urged upon a most impressionable group of young American expatriates simple truths about the writing of fiction:

You must therefore write as simply as you can—with the extreme of the simplicity that is granted to you, and you must write of subjects that spring at your throat. But why subjects appeal to you you have no means of knowing. The appeal of the subject is nevertheless the only thing that is open to your native genius —the only thing as to which you can say: "I cannot help it: that is what appealed to me!" You must never, after that, say: "I write like this because I want to," but you must say: "I write like this because it is what the unspoiled reader likes!"

iv

The occasion, of course, of this activity in Paris among young American writers was the war. It had brought them away from their Midwest or from their undergraduate careers at Eastern universities; it had exercised the charm of Paris as "the great laboratory of the spirit," and it had given them the incentive for earnest work in the study of the literary arts which no mere course or series of courses in an American university could have given them. The art of fiction was taught, not at the Sorbonne, but wherever Pound, or Ford, or Miss Stein conversed and advised. The war was also a supremely influential circumstance. Much of the talk by and about the "lost generation" was superficial and platitudinous, the result of a revolt that had quickly hardened into a few clichés. But the war had very genuinely the effect of cutting off the more acute and the more sensitive of these writers from the security of prewar generalizations and intellectual comforts. As John Peale Bishop has said in an illuminating essay, "The Missing All":

The most tragic thing about the war was not that it made so many dead men, but that it destroyed the tragedy of death. Not only did the young suffer in the war, but every abstraction that would have sustained and given dignity to their suffering. The war made the traditional morality inacceptable; it did not annihilate it; it revealed its immediate inadequacy. So that at its end, the survivors were left to face, as they could, a world without values.

Whatever the various modes of response to this fact (and there were many novels which exploited it as it led into a merely popular and profitable view), its effect upon both the attitude and the art of the postwar novelists was profound. There were, in fact, two important consequences for them: through the (often artificial) stimulus of the life in Paris, they were led into exciting and sometimes serious studies of the problems of fiction as an art; because of their distrust of the major generalizations of the prewar world, they were inclined to attend to the immediate nature of present experience and to work through to both a form and a meaning in literature from what was given in the record. There is little if any of the "imported" meaning, the borrowed interpretation of motives and acts, that one finds so often in the naturalist fiction at the turn of the century. If they were naïve, they were also far less pretentious than their predecessors. Of the nineteenth-century American novelists, only Mark Twain and Stephen Crane seemed to have had something to say to them, and the former principally because of his *Huckleberry Finn,* which had held, except for a few unfortunate lapses, honestly to the tone and to the limitations of its subject. To Crane they felt indebted for his honest attempt to account for and describe the genuine emotions stimulated by battle—this chiefly from *The Red Badge of Courage,* though some of the stories of *Wounds in the Rain* (1900) would probably have come closer to their own intention. Even in his important Civil War novel, Crane had often been clumsily "artistic" where Hemingway was rigidly faithful to his material. It is doing more than justice to Crane to compare the opening paragraph from *The Red Badge of Courage* with that of *A Farewell to Arms.* In each case we have a description of a war setting—a beginning of the war scene, with the natural detail serving symbolically to establish the tone of what follows:

The cold passed reluctantly from the earth, and the retiring fogs revealed an army stretched out on the hills, resting. As the landscape changed from brown to green, the army awakened, and began to tremble with eagerness at the noise of rumors. It cast its eyes upon the roads, which were growing from long troughs of liquid mud to proper thoroughfares. A river, amber-tinted in the shadow of its banks, purled at the army's feet; and at night, when the stream had become of a sorrowful blackness, one could see across it the red, eyelike gleam of hostile camp fires set in the low brows of distant hills. *(The Red Badge of Courage)*

* * *

In the late summer of that year we lived in a house in a village that looked across the river and the plain to the mountains. In the bed of the river there were pebbles and boulders, dry and white in the sun, and the water was clear and swiftly moving and blue in the channels. Troops went by the house and down the road and the dust they raised powdered the leaves of the trees. The trunks of the trees too were dusty and the leaves fell early that year and we saw the troops marching along the road and the dust rising and leaves, stirred by the breeze, falling and the soldiers marching and afterward the road bare and white except for the leaves. *(A Farewell to Arms)*

All of which is to say that the postwar novel was different in tone and manner from its predecessors. The young novelists had actually gone to school to their contemporaries and to those who were seriously concerned with their careers as artists. For all the eccentricity, the suspicion of posing, the false shouting and tumult, of these years in exile—the "avant-garde forever posing under its Picasso, and talking modernism with a Midwestern accent," as Kazin remarked— much was learned; what was learned had almost always to do with the actual writing and not with a theory that should impose upon and direct the writing. There are vast stretches of intellect and experience which separate James from Hemingway, Wharton from Fitzgerald. If they possessed less of James's and Wharton's acuteness of insight into their world, they had even a greater desire to perfect what talent they had. Much of their final work has a quality of improvisation about it, and much of their point of view has a certain naïve surprise in its limited excellence. But it might be said of them that they were almost always aware of their mistakes, that their successes came not accidentally (or laden with the reminders of early failures) but after very hard and persistent application.

5

THE AMERICAN NOVEL BETWEEN WARS

i

OF ALL the fiction that came from the war and from postwar experiences, that of Ernest Hemingway has been judged most representative. While, in the popular mind, Fitzgerald was identified with the very young generation—those twelve- to eighteen-year-olds who began to advise their elders and to set them an example—Hemingway had soon fixed himself in the attention of the returning soldier, who, like his Krebs, felt that "there was something wrong" in the world to which he had returned. It was not only the war itself that Hemingway had definitively characterized, but the postwar world as well—the world of the Paris expatriate. The image of the Jake Barnes-Bill Gorton-Lady Brett crowd, of what they did and of how they adjusted to the emergencies of a postwar situation, was soon established among a generation of readers who had read little or none of Henry James or Edith Wharton, and knew Howells not at all.

There were others who wrote war fiction. John Dos Passos had been first in the field, with his *One Man's Initiation: 1917* (1920) and *Three Soldiers* (1921). E. E. Cummings' autobiographical novel, *The Enormous Room,* had appeared in 1922. Thomas Boyd's *Through the Wheat* (1923) had given a thoroughly realistic account of the life of the common soldier in France. Any one of these novels was sufficient to offset the impression made by Edith Wharton's portrayal of the "crusade for civilization," in *The Marne* (1918) and *A Son at the Front* (1923), and the last section of Willa Cather's *One of Ours* (1922). What Percy Boynton has said of *One of Ours* may fairly well be said of all of these last-named novels:

The truth about warfare has been rediscovered of late. I have yet to find a soldier who has been long at the front who has read the book without a feeling of revulsion at the concluding chapters. Barbusse and Dos Passos, Remarque and Hemingway, are more likely to be to their taste. The death of Miss Cather's hero has been to them the snuffing of a candle rather than the apotheosis of a lover of democracy.

The horror and the boredom of the war were what the postwar generation wanted to discover for itself; they wished, moreover, to have the accounts of the war, not from the women of an earlier generation (twenty-two years separate the birth of Miss Cather from that of Hemingway), but from men who had been there and had fought in or at least experienced the war. The impression left by Dos Passos, Boyd, and Cummings was a strange mixture of the most unrelieved realism and a sentimental protest against violations of taste. For Dos Passos, the realism served to underscore the cry of violated youth; for Cummings, the grim details of life in a detention camp emphasized every step of the way the vast difference between vulgar officialdom and the pure and happy spirit of the best prisoners, the "Delectable Mountains" of his book.

The war served as a presiding background of all Hemingway's fiction in the 1920's; when, in 1929, *A Farewell to Arms* was published, he had already given the war definitive and sharply effective treatment. In the brief "interchapters" which served as thematic commentary upon the stories of *In Our Time* (1925), and in the portrait of Jake Barnes, war victim of *The Sun Also Rises,* readers had already found an eloquent portrayal of the war as both fact and effect. *A Farewell to Arms* thus gave a unified and continuous account of what had been done sporadically in earlier Hemingway books.

The language, the dialogue and the design of *A Farewell to Arms,* had already been prepared for. A convention of war literature had been established, by Hemingway and his contemporaries. The stark literalness of Boyd's descriptions and dialogue in *Through the Wheat,* the antiheroics of Dos Passos (as well as his portrayal of the deserter's "separate peace"), the restrained and unemotional descriptions of war in *In Our Time*—these had sufficiently prepared readers for the genuinely effective "Caporetto" section of *A Farewell to Arms.* Throughout this work there had been a frequent reaction against the "holy abstractions" of Western civilization, which, in the midst of trench warfare and melancholy retreats, seemed a culminating profanity against the dignity of man. The effect of all this was reductive and intellectually disenchanting. In the war literature of the 1920's, writers proudly displayed the irony of war facts contrasted with arm-chair heroics. A precedent for this had, of course, been provided in Crane's portrait of Henry Fleming's ordeal. What made Hemingway important was that from these beginnings he had made a careful and a conscientious formula for the art of the novel. This meant that he had not merely exploited the war theme or carefully cultivated the advantages of the readers' acquired tastes, but had honestly worked within his own experience and developed its possibilities. His material *was* his experience, and he had only to resist the temptation to make it something less than honestly his own in order to gain success and financial security. As Bishop has said, "Toward his craft, he was humble, and had, moreover, the most complete literary integrity it has ever been my lot to encounter. I say the most complete, for while I have known others who were not to be corrupted, none of them was presented with the opportunities for corruption that assailed Hemingway."

He had brought to Paris with him in 1922 the experiences of a Midwesterner and the haphazard training which a few years as a newspaper reporter had given him. He had also a profound distrust of all literary talent, including his own. There was a difference between reporting and literature, and he proceeded to discover just what that difference involved for him, in hard work and discipline. He learned that difference from Pound, and Ford, and Gertrude Stein. Pound blue-penciled his early work, struck out most of the adjectives and gave its latent clarity a chance to become explicit. With her advice, Miss Stein helped him to retain and develop a simplicity of expression which had before her been largely an accident resulting from his freedom from academic influences. As Bishop puts it, "Miss Stein had developed a literary medium; but she had no material, at least none that was available to that strangely infantile genius of hers."

All of Hemingway's experiences were ideally suited to the development of his kind of fictional art. The themes to which he had recourse were not literary at all, but a part of the naïve wonder and perplexity of a "pure and ignorant spirit" in the modern world. His fiction of the 1920's was a continuous record or reminder of the need to adjust to the complexity and the violence of that world. On the one hand there were the comforts and the excitements of Nick Adams' life in the northern Michigan woods; on the other, there was a collection and variety of experiences almost totally alien to them. The two contrasting worlds were put in sharp juxtaposition in *In Our Time*. The impersonal death and destruction described in the "Chapters" could have no meaning save what it gained from such an arrangement. Before the story "Indian Camp," for example, we have the sketch of a group of soldiers on the road to the Champagne: "The whole battery was drunk going along the road in the dark." Immediately following the story of Nick Adams, "Chapter II" provides a starkly impersonal account of refugees fleeing a city in the Near East:

. . . There was no end and no beginning. Just carts loaded with everything they owned. The old men and women, soaked through, walked along keeping the cattle moving. . . . The women and children were in the carts, crouched with mattresses, mirrors, sewing machines, bundles. There was a woman having a baby with a young girl holding a blanket over her and crying. Scared sick looking at it. It rained all through the evacuation.

The story placed between these two sketches describes Nick Adams's introduction to both birth and death—both "an end and a beginning." Nick's father is forced to resort to a caesarian operation in order to deliver the Indian woman's child. The procedure is dignified and accompanied by a quiet professional pride, as he explains it simply to Nick. The Indian father, unable to bear the torture of his wife's screams and the fear that she may die, kills himself. Nick as observer of this beginning and this end, needs his father's reassuring explanation in order to assimilate what he has learned:

> "Is dying hard, daddy?"
> "No, I think it's pretty easy, Nick. It all depends." They were seated in the boat, Nick in the stern, his father rowing. The sun was coming up over the hils. A bass jumped, making a circle in the water. Nick trailed his hand in the water. It felt warm in the sharp chill of the morning.
> In the early morning on the lake sitting in the stern of the boat with his father rowing, he felt quite sure that he would never die.

The elements of contrast are all starkly given: the dying and the birth have contrasting meanings and settings in the two alternating accounts; the new consciousness of the young boy contrasts sharply with that of the observer in the two "chapters"; in the two settings are contained all of the violent dislocations of experience and sensibility which were a part of Hemingway's own life. In other parts of *In Our Time* the contrasting worlds have much the same effect. The protection given Nick by his parents is insufficient preparation for his move to the world outside, beyond the woods. There is something discernibly unsatisfactory about his mother's Christian Science and her cheerful evasiveness, and his father also proves to be an inadequate protector.

This pervasive contrast and its impression on Nick Adams

are what goes into the making of Jake Barnes and Lieutenant Henry. There is in each case a denial of the validity of
any but direct experience. There is nothing in the world of
ideas that either sustains the Hemingway hero or provides
him with a formula of rejection. For such an uncomplex
sensibility as Hemingway's, there is no intellectual activity
such as animated the decisions of other war heroes: Alding-
ton's, for example, in *Death of a Hero;* Dos Passos' Martin
Howe of *One Man's Initiation* or John Andrews of *Three
Soldiers;* or Ford's Tietjens. Nevertheless Hemingway's
work moves inevitably toward a formularization of attitude
and reaction. This takes the form of a carefully developed
symbolic ritual, borrowed from the sports in which Hemingway was most interested. These sports have rules which must
be scrupulously followed; they also demand a setting, an
atmosphere, which cannot be violated, or they lose their
usefulness. For *In Our Time* the sport is fishing, under
the circumstances described in the two "Big Two-Hearted
River" stories which come at the end of that book. That
sport is replaced in *The Sun Also Rises* by bullfighting,
chiefly because fishing is no longer equal to the task of providing an orderly pattern of the kind of experience described in that novel. A fishing trip of Jake Barnes and
Bill Gorton's in *The Sun Also Rises* is brilliantly told, but
it is obvious now that Hemingway cannot trust it for more
than the idyllic interlude that it is. A telegram reaches them,
and they must return to unsolved problems and unresolved
tensions which the fishing trip had merely helped them to
evade.

As we discover in the Pamplona chapters of *The Sun
Also Rises* and in *Death in the Afternoon* (1932), the bullfight has the several advantages over every other sport used
by Hemingway in his fiction: it involves the risk of death;

both the danger and the evidence of death are continuously and often conspicuously present throughout; it is, moreover, a carefully formulated work of art—or, as Hemingway puts it, a three-act drama; finally, it so challenges the skill, courage, and art of the bullfighter that it is easy for the *aficionado* to mark the difference between the real thing and faking.

Romero never made any contortions, always it was straight and pure and natural in line. The others twisted themselves like corkscrews, their elbows raised, and leaned against the flanks of the bull after his horns had passed, to give a faked look of danger. Afterward, all that was faked turned bad and gave an unpleasant feeling. Romero's bull-fighting gave real emotion, because he kept the absolute purity of line in his movements and always quietly and calmly let the horns pass him close each time . . . Romero had the old thing, the holding of his purity of line through the maximum of exposure, while he dominated the bull by making him realize he was unattainable, while he prepared him for the killing.

This discussion, as well as the others in *The Sun Also Rises,* are a crucial part of the novel's design and meaning. The bullfight serves as both a contrasting design and a challenge to the behavior of Jake's friends. The Paris scenes which begin the novel, in their description of expatriates in the bars, convey the ugliness and hopelessness of defeat. The defeat is both suggested by the vulgarization of manners (Brett's entering, accompanied by homosexuals, the irritating romanticism of Cohn) and the futility of Jake's and Brett's love. This kind of existence has only accidental definition, and the sole defense against it seems to be the slick, evasive wisecrack. The movement of this group toward Pamplona is temporarily interrupted by the fishing expedition at Burguete; here the wisecracking continues,

and to it is added the now specious pleasure of the quiet
stream, the wine, and the fishing itself.

In Pamplona the tensions which are for the most part
lost in the Paris scenes are intensified. Hemingway's portrayal of these tensions, of their causes and their culmination
in violation, is masterful. It is all very ugly. The violence
and the drunkenness come as an unsatisfactory adjustment
to a situation that is desperately unhappy. "I'm drunk, I
tell you, mon vieux. Oh, I am soused," the lieutenant had
said in the first sketch of *In Our Time*. The drinking in
The Sun Also Rises is undertaken for the same reasons and
under what may be described as similar circumstances. The
quarreling and drinking of Jake's friends take place in the
setting of a religious festival and the bullfighting. The religious anniversary serves for the most part as an excuse for
merriment, but even it contains a symbolic meaning for the
natives which is embarrassedly rejected by Jake and Brett
on their few visits to the church. The services for the man
who has been killed in the *desencajonada* provide the simple security that protects his survivors from the ugly facts
of death. But it is in the bullfighting itself and in the art
as practised by Pedro Romero that the progress of Jake's
friends from Paris to Pamplona is most fully and devastat-
ingly characterized. While these two major themes of the
novel exist mainly in contrast, there is a significant way in
which they join: through Jake's friendship with Montoya
the life of Romero is eventually defiled by contact with the
world of Brett. She has, in the end, a glimmering of what
Romero's life and art mean, and she leaves him in order
to save him from her world.

As a consequence of this skillful organization of Hemingway's expatriate world, the genuine honesty of purpose is
made effectively clear. It is not the dispersion of meaning,

the collapse of it into a huge bawdy hopeless joke that Hemingway intends here, but rather the moral imperative which total isolation from the world of his immediate past has forced upon them. That isolation is brilliantly suggested: in the brief exchange that Jake has with the conventional, suburb-dwelling fellow correspondents, Woolsey and Krum; in the purposely slick comedy of Gorton and the American tourists in the train; in the helpless embarrassment of Jake's behavior inside the church; and, finally, in the pathetic comedy of the vulgar and noisy intrusion upon the Pamplona celebrations. The novel is furthermore a masterpiece in its honest competence with respect to the use of its materials.

Coming as it did both after *The Sun Also Rises* and at the end of the first postwar decade, *A Farewell to Arms* was in a position to exploit a considerable advantage. His readers were ready for him to provide a definitive novel about the war. In a very real sense, *A Farewell to Arms* bases its true value on retrospection; that is, the postwar situation of *The Sun Also Rises* arouses expectation for a novel which might explain, not the emotions of Jake and his crowd, but the historical origins of those emotions. Hemingway did certainly make the most of this opportunity; but in the end it must be said that *A Farewell to Arms* is scarcely the novel that might ideally have come from the author of *The Sun Also Rises*. The love affair of Lieutenant Henry and Catherine Barkley gains its chief value because of its setting. Its sentimentality and romantic softness are melodramatically touched by an amateurish philosophy. The descriptions of war, especially those of the retreat from Caporetto, have not been equalled by any other novelist, nor by Hemingway himself in any other of his works. But in this novel certain crudities appear which are not evident in his earlier work.

He is slowly but perceptibly losing hold of the discipline learned in the early years in Paris. The several passages in which Henry states, not his immediate impressions but what has to pass for a philosophical interpretation of them, never quite emerge as either suitable or necessary. Set alongside the eminently successful portrait of the Italian surgeon, Rinaldi, and the moderately successful delineation of the priest, there are the almost embarrassingly naïve conversations of Henry with the priest and with Count Greffi. What these people say to Henry is important, of course; and Hemingway had certainly intended the conversations to bear crucially the burden of the novel's meaning. But there is a note of softness and insincerity in the sentiments expressed, as in the manner of expressing them, which is all but absent from *The Sun Also Rises*. Briefly, the structure of *A Farewell to Arms* contains this formal meaning: that Henry, having for the vaguest of reasons joined the Italian forces during the war, finds its values unattractive and ugly and rejects them when the opportunity arises; that through his love for Catherine he is enabled not only to effect but also to justify his rejection of them; that, finally, having put all his hopes in the continuing satisfaction of that love, he finds himself at the end with nothing left. The love motif in the novel moves from the "game of chess" of the beginning, to the secular consecration that is blessed in the cynically sentimental dialogue with Count Greffi, to the final despairing and whining plea at the end of the novel, with all of the images and philosophical statement of an intellectual amateur lending its pathos to the culminating scene.

The observations of Lieutenant Henry which are most often quoted are given at the beginning of the Caporetto section; they at least have a dramatic place and may therefore be said to be justified in terms of the novel itself. They are, furthermore, in themselves most skillfully done. It is possible that Lieutenant Henry could have made them under the circumstances:

I was always embarrassed by the words sacred, glorious, and sacrifice and the expression in vain. We had heard them, sometimes standing in the rain almost out of earshot, so that only the shouted words came through, and had read them, on proclamations that were slapped up by billposters over other proclamations, now for a long time, and I had seen nothing sacred, and the things that were glorious had no glory and the sacrifices were like the stockyards at Chicago if nothing was done with the meat except to bury it.

What has happened to Hemingway between the time of this statement and the one which follows is a half-conversion to an ideological religion and a degeneration of moral insight and artistic integrity. Robert Jordan of *For Whom the Bell Tolls* (1940) is a descendant, not of Frederic Henry, but of Harry Morgan of *To Have and Have Not* (1937) and of the hero of Hemingway's loyalist play, *The Fifth Column* (1938). The nonfictional works of the intervening years, *Death in the Afternoon* (1932) and *The Green Hills of Africa* (1935), reveal an irritating tendency toward pseudo-heroic poses and insincerity. The earnest student of the craft of writing seems in these later books to have suffered the calamity of too much success.

Since when did you ever have any such conception? [Robert Jordan says to himself, concerning his love for Maria in "a purely materialistic conception of society."] Never. And you never could have. You're not a real Marxist and you know it. You believe in Liberty, Equality, and Fraternity. You believe in Life, Liberty and the Pursuit of Happiness. . . . You have put many things in abeyance to win a war. If this war is lost all of those things are lost.

The sacrifices are no longer "in vain." The words which "embarrassed" Lieutenant Henry (which, indeed, angered him when they were spoken by the *carabiniere*) now seem quite satisfactory as mental sanctions for quietly heroic behavior. In *For Whom the Bell Tolls* the action is always accompanied, implicitly or explicitly, by a slick ideological apologetic. Henry reacts with exasperation, then with numbness, to the sacrifice of Catherine; Jordan urges Maria to go away, from the scene at which he knows he will meet his death, with a solacing reminder of their spiritual oneness: "As long as there is one of us there is both of us. Do you understand?" Ray West has called this remark "the end of despair and futility—the end of the 'lost generation.'" What are the reasons for it?

Hemingway's chief virtue was his dedication to the art of writing within his own candidly recognized limitations. He was not a man of ideas, and he scorned those of his contemporaries who forced their experiences into pseudo-intellectual patterns or imposed ideas upon them. His misfortune was that the total impression of the work of the 1920's added up to nothing positive, and that he felt at the end of that decade that "something positive" was necessary. That feeling is more than indicated in the concluding remarks of Harry Morgan, who has lost his fight for independence; it is articulated as well in the contrasts drawn between Morgan and the idle rich or the merely idle. Hemingway had therefore taken hold of an idea, which, in the course of the 1930's fiction, underwent a number of changes. *To Have and Have Not* expresses it simply as the need for co-operation, and that need is abundantly if crudely documented;[1] the play,

1 *To Have and Have Not* is not a failure of conception but a failure of style. In it, Hemingway was victimized for the only time by the widespread experimenting in style and method that followed in the wake of *Ulysses* and *USA*.

The Fifth Column, gives it a candid and starkly leftist quality; *For Whom the Bell Tolls* returns it to the only cultural setting Hemingway could naturally have given it: that of the American tradition which he understood only in its catch phrases. In addition, the respect for aesthetic integrity which he had learned at the beginning of his career had now been fairly well dissipated in the pretentious conversations with the "Old Lady" of *Death in the Afternoon* and the Austrian hunter of *The Green Hills of Africa;* from being a humble worker in the art of fiction, he had now become a rather too authoritative critic of modern literature.

The theme of *For Whom the Bell Tolls* is not unrelated to his earlier interests. The Spaniards in the Pamplona crowds of *The Sun Also Rises* are in the later novel more clearly individualized. They are realized brilliantly and effectively, and Hemingway demonstrates both his warmth of affection for them and his intimate understanding of them. Its major significance is not in the failure of idiom but in the confusion of sentiment and meaning which makes for a vitiating and falsifying ideological use of the materials of the novel.

The contribution of Hemingway to modern fiction can best be inferred from what he has done by way of establishing and exploring exhaustively the possibilities of simplicity. The "esthetic of simplicity" involves not merely a specious fidelity to Howells's commonplace truth but a basic struggle for absolute accuracy in making words correspond to experience. In this struggle the absence of intellectual interest, his scorn of men who "make abstractions do for experience," served him well. The problems of structure and style had all therefore to be related to discrete and irreducible fact, unencumbered (or scarcely ever encumbered) by falsely imposed meanings and organized into intrinsically meaningful structures. What had served him so well in the 1920's, however, forced him in the 1930's to have recourse to a body of intellectual discourse to which his 1920's writing had shown him temperamentally allergic.

ii

A portion of the fiction of the 1920's was indebted to a body of learning and science which merits a peculiar distinction in the history of modern American mores. The path of psychoanalysis from Vienna to Greenwich Village was a straight one if not true. It was not only the very active suggestions that Freud had made to young novelists that made its influence widespread; psychoanalysis came into the American consciousness because American writers were more than ready for it. It seemed a ready-made scientific explanation and extenuation of the American life, as these writers had seen it. From 1910 to 1930, there was a steady growth in curiosity regarding all of the secret recesses of explanation for the sex life. This was a part of the revolt of youth against their elders. In social criticism it acquired the strange and interesting form of a half-scientific, half-imaginative investigation of the devastating consequences for modern America of the Puritan conscience: Waldo Frank's *Our America* (1919), Harvey O'Higgins' *The American Mind in Action* (1924) Matthew Josephson's *Portrait of the Artist as American* (1930), Ludwig Lewisohn's autobiographical versions of American cultural history, Van Wyck Brooks's biographies of Mark Twain and Henry James—these were, each in its own way, documents in the history of the American moral crisis.

More specifically, the suggestions of the new psychology had a very noticeable influence upon the attitudes which novelists took toward their work. There were examples in abundance of every one of the crucial ideas which Freud had early offered to American readers in *The Interpretation of Dreams* (1913) and *Three Contributions to a Theory of Sex* (1918), translated by A. A. Brill. Yet there is no American novel in this group that is much more than historically interesting. The "experiments" are ingenious and different but largely shallow and naïve. As they were in Europe, the modern extensions and elaborations of the so-called "stream of consciousness" technique were in abundant evidence; and these existed in combination with a precocious examination of American sex life, normal, abnormal, and otherwise. In its particular literary applications, it took the form of further and further elaborations of the "dream consciousness." The dream state or the condition of revery became more and more important as the crucial means of developing a narrative. The dream state had its own kinds of subtlety, and its uses for social criticism.

The more elaborate uses of the stream of consciousness were in no small measure related to the success which Joyce's *Ulysses* had had in America many years before Judge Woolsey's court decision in 1936 made the sale of that novel legal. Conrad Aiken's *Blue Voyage* (1927) was the American novel most conspicuously indebted to Joyce, as his *Great Circle* (1933) was the American example of the Freudian substance invading the novel's range of characterization. But there were other, and more distinctively American, developments of each: the explorations undertaken by Waldo Frank, for example, of a peculiarly static and vague subliminal world, in *Rahab* (1922), *City Block* (1922), and *Chalk Face* (1924); the exploitation of the unconscious for purposes of cultural criticism, in Frank's *Holiday* (1923); and the use of a mixture of psychological analysis and religious insight in the

same author's *The Death and Birth of David Markand*
(1934). As for the pervasive and notorious applications of
Freud's discussions of the sexual life, these were an important part of a general revision of sexual attitudes during the
postwar period. Miss Bronte had discreetly kept Rochester's
wife imprisoned for her abnormality; it served her author
dramatically because of that isolation; Ellen Glasgow permitted her distressed females a place at table and used them
as an ever-present reminder of the critical failure of a traditional manner. But for a novelist like Evelyn Scott, the
neurotic suffered the stages of her progress toward psychosis
in full view of her relatives and readers. *The Narrow House*
(1921) and *Narcissus* (1922) give us a collection of people
whose neurotic behavior is analyzed with a distressing
thoroughness and portrayed with all of the ugliness and
none of the affections associated with the "romantic passion." What happens to them is in part ascribed to the ugly
and dogmatic ignorance which a great majority of the postwar novelists seemed to find in their elders. This criticism
of the neo-Puritan stereotype was also attached to the frontal
assault upon his laws, which apparently suffered from a
similar ignorance of the natural and instinctual life. The
word "convention" became a most convenient scapegoat for
all of the bitter laughter in which postwar novelists indulged
at the expense of their innocent elders. The love that sur-
passeth all understanding had certainly been misunderstood
by the upholders of a conventional morality. Nor had the
older generation quite understood the need for freedom in
sexual experiment, which existed beyond and outside of
institutional blessings and taboos. Thus we have an exten-
sive record, in the fiction of Ludwig Lewisohn, of an im-
passioned protest against the divorce laws, in *The Case of
Mr. Crump* (1926) and in *Stephen Escott* (1930). All of this

fiction was a deadly earnest expression of reproach, made articulate in a decade when sexual crises seemed far more important than threat of war or depression.

It is also intimately associated with another theme, the reverse of the pastoral motif. Carl Van Doren had dubbed it "The Revolt from the Village" in his discussion of Edgar Lee Masters and others. For such novelists as Floyd Dell the city was the shining goal of adolescent hope. The sensitive soul who had suffered a steam bath of repression in the hinterlands of the Midwest, experienced an immediate release upon his arrival in Chicago. From there, he proceeded to New York, and often to Paris, in search of better and better bohemian refuges. No one has left a more sentimental reminiscence of Greenwich Village than Mr. Dell, nor did any other American novelist explore with quite his indefatigable interest the possibilities for fiction of illicit love sentimentally described and defended.

The major symptomatic gesture of this fiction had its precedent in Sherwood Anderson's dramatic and romanticized "walking out" from his business office in Elyria, Ohio. We find it explained in his autobiographical books, such as *A Story-Teller's Story* (1924), and used as a climactic gesture in many of his novels. His heroes almost invariably prove their distaste for society by leaving it and by making a meaningful ceremony of their going. Of course, for George Willard in *Winesburg, Ohio* (1919), the going is not so much a protest as it is the beginning of fulfilment; his manhood as well as his career is at stake. Sam McPherson of *Windy McPherson's Son* (1916) abruptly leaves the commercial world so that he may "spend his life seeking truth." In *Many Marriages* (1922), John Webster turns away from his business and his family, convinced that both are morally incompetent and potentially evil. His departure is a climactic act in the pattern of Anderson's "Out of Nowhere into Nothing." In other novels, reasons are given for the divorce of man from the business world. As Lionel Trilling wrote, in explanation of the Preface to *Winesburg, Ohio:*

It was the truth—or perhaps we must call it a simple complex of truths—of love-passion-freedom, and it was made up of these "vague thoughts": that each individual is a precious secret essence, often discordant with all other essences; that society, and more particularly the industrial society, threatens these essences; that the old good values of life have been destroyed by the industrial dispensation; that people have been cut off from each other and even from themselves.

What made all of this so terribly important in the 1920's was the deadly earnestness with which Anderson developed his fictional explanations of this complex of truths. Anderson was a man with a mission and he tried sincerely and repetitiously to recommend himself as a serious missionary. His criticism of the industrial demon led him to the creation of simple angels. Their most highly intelligent act was their groping toward profound truths, from which each fashioned his own grotesque. The individual inadequacies of these people added up to a huge and grotesque inadequacy located at the heart of modern American society. Anderson's characters find no relief in Floyd Dell's bohemias; they are, in fact, illiterate, unlettered, and inarticulate, striving desperately and vainly for a verbal equivalent of their feelings. It is only occasionally that they can find such an equivalent; but when they do, as do Sponge Martin and Bruce Dudley of *Dark Laughter* (1925), they become not only articulate but garrulous.

The range and meaning of Anderson's protest found their

most successful expression in *Poor White* (1920). Here, in the character of the almost dumbly shy Hugh McVey is a veritable stereotype of pre-industrial man. The irony of the narrative lies in his having perfected a machine for the planting of cabbages because he desperately wants to save the poor laborers in the cabbage fields from their back-breaking work. From this motive, therefore, and not from a lust for power and wealth, McVey becomes an inventor and a servant of the industrial world. He destroys the beauty of Bidwell, which changes from a pleasant small town into an ugly industrial center. Throughout these distressing experiences McVey remains a shy, gentle creature, free of the brutalizing effects of wealth and the temptations of power. At the novel's end he is able to sum up his experience and the town's, using his own unwitting contribution to its corruption as the unholy example.

This novel contributes the simplification of a thesis which is present implicitly or overtly in many of its contemporaries. The thesis embraces Freudian influences as it does social and historical criticisms. The simple, natural soul is one of the victims of a soulless and vulgar materialism; in its primitive habitat, and in such survivals as the Negroes, it had enjoyed the virtues of a simple and unsubtle sincerity; but the advantages of materialism are gained at the sacrifice of man's nobler impulses, which are repressed almost to the point of extinction. The survivor of this holocaust is apparently a man who either remains remarkably simple in spite of overpowering odds against his chances, or the man who "has had enough" and who walks out on the world, endlessly explaining and glorifying his decision.

Anderson had, in fact, made a virtue of his own lack of subtlety. He defended his work chiefly on the grounds that simple truths need no more than a literal transcription, even

when they acquire complexity through distortion into gro-
tesques.

For a long time I have believed that crudity is an inevitable
quality in the production of a really significant present-day
American literature [he wrote in 1916]. How indeed is one to
escape the obvious fact that there is as yet no native subtlety of
thought or living among us? And if we are a crude and childlike
people how can our literature hope to escape the influence of
that fact? Why indeed should we want it to escape?

This defense of what is substantially an unintellectual
point of view was not without its justification in Anderson's
world. There was a whole-hearted repudiation of subtlety,
which, along with an undiscriminating enthusiasm for reading, established a current of literary attitude in twentieth-
century fiction. As a form of realism it was both naïve
and artless. The mysterious fascination of words and vague
thoughts of which Anderson so often spoke in his critical
pieces was a precious motivation for this kind of writing.
The words came together in a kind of unconscious process
of creative illiteracy and left the thoughts free of damaging
subtlety—indeed, created their own brand of subtlety, in
their confused meandering among the subconscious will
and mind. It is of course true that none of Anderson's
"minds" deserved the subtlety of rendering given hers by
Virginia Woolf. But Anderson could have had only a damning consequence for American letters through his having
provided a constant justification for crudity and made a
virtue of it. Only if taken seriously, of course; but who did
not take him seriously in the 1920's? The fundamental difference between Anderson and Hemingway is a difference
in attitude toward the art of writing. Both, as we know, sat
at the feet of Gertrude Stein. But Anderson brought what

he knew and took nothing away, and Hemingway learned the hard lessons of the discipline of writing fiction, in the profitable realization that the art demanded more than perfect sentences. Anderson expanded from these sentences into themes vaguely but urgently developed into novels. The themes acquired the quality of the "vague thoughts" which everywhere dominated his vision of his own experiences: the vision of "the great renunciation," for one, and its resulting views of industrial Philistia and its hapless victims; the persistently earnest search, for another, in naïve symbols for the verbal equivalent of dimly known feelings. "From the wonder of that escape," says Trilling of his departure from Elyria, "he seems never to have recovered, and his continued pleasure in it did him harm, for it seems to have made him feel that the problem of the artist was defined wholly by the struggle between sincerity on the one hand and commercialism and gentility on the other. He did indeed say that the artist needed not only courage but craft, yet it was surely the courage by which he set the most store."

iii

No longer imitative and timorous, as most of their predecessors were, these youngsters are attempting a first-hand examination of the national scene, and making an effort to represent it in terms that are wholly American. They are the pioneers of a literature that, whatever its defects in the abstract, will at least be a faithful reflection of the national life, that will be more faithful, indeed, in its defects than in its merits.

—H. L. M.

The youngsters whom Henry L. Mencken admired were Sinclair Lewis, Willa Cather, James Branch Cabell, and Joseph Hergesheimer. His admiration of them was based

on what he himself believed a "first-hand examination of
the national scene" should reveal. That critical sense which
had seemed so important in the second and third decades
of the century was limited to a few principles of judgment
and selection. He did not by any means like everything of
Miss Cather's; nor was he especially wise in having singled
out Hergesheimer for special mention. What Mencken did
for the fiction of the 1920's was to establish a climate of
acceptance in which a certain kind of writing could flourish.
That this was varied enough is testified to in its inclusion
of two widely different novelists, Cabell and Lewis. In short,
this fiction had either to present a gross parody of middle-
class manners or to give rein to a fantasy which in its very
extreme shut out that class. Partly the object was to shock—
as had been Mencken's in much of his own writing. Though
he approved of Miss Cather's portrayal of the native scene,
he was more interested in what he saw as Lewis's kindred
talent for mockery and burlesque. He was also fond of the
literature which suffered persecution from the successors of
Comstock and other leaders of what he had called in 1917
"militant Puritanism." Cabell's persecution by these people
(his *Jurgen* was banned by The New York Society for the
Supression of Vice) lifted him from merited obscurity to
fame, and as he had done with Dreiser, Mencken gloried
in the opportunity to defend another victim of the "boo-
boisie."

Closest to Mencken in the 1920's was Sinclair Lewis. To
both, the behavior of the middle class had appeared to be,
superficially at least, an endlessly amusing spectacle. In the
case of Lewis, the successes of the 1920's combined the merits
of both style and subject-matter. Lewis found at least one
part of his subject in *Main Street* (1920); with that his career
got its real start, mainly because the work of Mencken and

his like had made the public eager and ready for this kind of novel. It was ready to accept Carol Kennicott not for Lewis's art but for the precision of effect with which she came to them as a familiar person. As *Main Street* became the standard exposition of the small town, so *Babbitt,* which followed in 1922, provided the all-sufficient portrait of the hustling, growing small city, with all of the folklore and folksay and mythology of the modern middle-class world. No American novel of this period enjoyed so widespread an esteem, and no novelist had ever discovered so happily or exploited so thoroughly this rich source of popular appeal. The natural consequence was that he continued to exploit it. So *Arrowsmith* (1925) contained some of *Main Street* and some of *Babbitt,* as well as a number of other things; *Elmer Gantry* (1927) was *Babbitt* with its collar turned; *The Man Who Knew Coolidge* (1928) was a succession of monologues in which all of the most compelling of middle-class views, clichés, and illusions were richly displayed; and it was only in *Dodsworth* (1929) that Lewis's opinions began to suggest clearly his genuine attitude toward his hero. In this last novel, Sam Dodsworth wins both the affection and the respect of his readers simply through the homely frankness and the refreshing naïveté of his point of view. Lewis could keep his audience when he openly showed his admiration of Dodsworth as well as when he had reveled in the patent absurdities of Babbitt.

These are the novels on which Lewis's fame fairly rests. Their success was a masterpiece of literary strategy, more thorough than had been Fitzgerald's phenomenally opportune exploitation of another vein of the 1920's lode. In this review of American life, Lewis enjoyed the eager accommodation and the close co-operation of Mencken—whose taste put *The Man Who Knew Coolidge* in a higher rank

than critics have since given it. But Lewis's work was not
mere journalism. He made as much of an art of his portrayal
as it was within his capacity to do. This art consisted partly
of sensitivity to every one of the clichés of sentiment and
public attitude which Mencken so enthusiastically collected
for the "Americana" section of the *Mercury*. Put together
and dramatized as they were in *Babbitt* and its successors,
they provided a parody-fantasy of the American middle
class: an unreal world made up of fragments of the socially
real, a montage of editorials, speeches, and advertisements.
This is the greatest contribution Lewis made to the postwar
novel, and it is what will give *Babbitt* a place in literature
long after Mencken's "Americana" are forgotten. In it all
of the attractions of the literally real but fantastic world
exist in an undeniably fascinating whole. While Mencken
had wanted his researches into American stupidity to document a thesis which he believed in with an intense mock-
seriousness, Lewis's work was not documentation at all, but
a variety of the fictional art. No Nietzsche or Darwin lurked
behind the scenes, but the comic spirit, and it survived only
so long as Lewis was prepared to allow it. Even Babbitt's
"Fairy Child" was permissible so long as she remained a
part of the comedy. It is only when she, along with Paul
Riesling and Seneca Doane began to intrude with a sentimental earnestness of purpose that the effect of *Babbitt* was
marred. Of all of Lewis's work, in fact, only *The Man Who
Knew Coolidge* is "pure Lewis," that is, an unadulterated
review of the materials upon which he exercised his comic
imagination. The materials themselves constituted one of
the most important sources for the modern satirical novel,
and in his best moments Lewis did at least point to its possibilities.

A mere reiteration of evidence does not make for the most

telling use of such advantages. The use of it needs to be creative and to contain a unified setting and atmosphere which give it meaning and continuity. These are what Lewis provided in his Zenith, state of Winnemac, the growingest, zippiest, hustlingest burg in the grand old Republican U. S. A. The vigor of Lewis's writing was equal to the energy of his imaginary synthesis of American hustle. In his skill in integrating the character of Babbitt with the world of Zenith, Lewis scored a minor triumph. But he was not pure parodist; he was also a skeptic and a liberal—that is, he shared vaguely that strangely defeatist liberalism of the 1920's that, shaken, had survived the destruction of Upton Sinclair's Helicon Hall. And he was middle class; some of his best friends were Babbitts. His intelligence prevented him from making the unhappy mistake which vitiates almost all of the leftist satires of the 1930's. But the progress of his middle-class hero from Babbitt to Dodsworth was not convincing because too earnestly gullible in the very manner that the creatures of his best novels were gullible. Babbitt moved in this sequence from Zenith, not to Mark Twain's Washington but to Gary Cooper's Hollywood. The clichés, if they still did not sound true after *Dodsworth*, were at least defended warmly, with an apologetic strength of affection which demonstrated that Lewis hadn't really meant *Babbitt* at all—or, rather, that he had genuinely preferred the tender, fearful Babbitt of the moments with Paul Riesling to the confident Babbitt of the after-dinner speeches and the conventions. *Work of Art* (1934) gave the business world a status it had not had in the novels of the 1920's; it had become literally a "work of art." *It Can't Happen Here* (1935) showed Lewis at his most sentimentally "liberal," applauding the homespun political tradition which in the end counter-attacked the Zenith state of mind and preserved America from its worst implications. *Gideon Planish* (1943), *Cass Timberlane* (1945), and *Kingsblood Royal* (1947), the novels which follow, show a continuous decline of powers and an irritable indecision concerning the meaning of what he is doing.

At its best, Lewis's writing shows a remarkable concentration upon the singleness of its effect: the caricature of manners and scenes is eminently appropriate and right—as, for example, in this description of the Zenith Athletic Club:

The entrance lobby of the Athletic Club was Gothic, the washroom Roman Imperial, the lounge Spanish Mission, and the reading-room in Chinese Chippendale, but the gem of the club was the dining-room, the masterpiece of Ferdinand Reitman, Zenith's busiest architect. It was lofty and half-timbered, with Tudor leaded casements, an oriel, a somewhat musicianless musicians'-gallery, and tapestries believed to illustrate the granting of Magna Charta. The open beams had been hand-adzed at Jake Offutt's car-body works, the hinges were of hand-wrought iron, the wainscot studded with hand-made wooden pegs, and at one end of the room was a heraldic and hooded stone fireplace which the club's advertising-pamphlet asserted to be not only larger than any of the fireplaces in European castles but of a draught incomparably more scientific. It was also much cleaner, as no fire had ever been built in it.

This is an ingenious caricature-summary of all of the pretensions of Athletic Club architecture the country over.[2] It is just that power of synthesis that makes it extraordinarily effective—as are Lewis's patterns of opinion and slogan, and characterizations such as that of Chum Frink. But his weaknesses are revealed precisely in those moments when he abandons this kind of opportunity, or when the narrative

2 A comparable effect is gained in Nathanael West's description of the horrors of Southern California domestic architectural styles, in *Day of the Locust* (1939), pp. 29–30.

strategy requires something else. Under these circumstances, he writes as badly as Sherwood Anderson at his feeble worst, and unwittingly provides his own clichés. The following, from the early section of *Main Street* (before Carol's move to Gopher Prairie) is an example:

From the cliffs across the river Carol and Kennicott looked back at St. Paul on its hills; an imperial sweep from the dome of the cathedral to the dome of the state capitol.

. . . .

. . . They climbed the hill to the round stone tower of Fort Snelling. They saw the junction of the Mississippi and the Minnesota, and recalled the men who had come here eighty years ago—Maine lumbermen, York traders, soldiers from the Maryland hills.
   "It's a good country, and I'm proud of it. Let's make it all that those old boys dreamed about," the unsentimental Kennicott was moved to vow.
   "Let's!"
   "Come on. Come to Gopher Prairie. Show us. Make the town —well—make it artistic. It's mighty pretty, but I'll admit we aren't any too darn artistic. Probably the lumberyard isn't as scrumptious as all these Greek temples. But go to it! Make us change!"

The point of view and the art of James Branch Cabell were both quite different from Lewis's; in fact, where Lewis was praised for his boisterous, good-humored satire, Cabell received applause for the delicacy and charm of his language and the precious grace of his imaginary creations. Cabell's association with the Mencken school of writers was, therefore, based on his quite different virtues. Lewis had, at his best, created a fantasy out of the real; Cabell's purposely designed fantasy-world was made up of a tissue of devices to reject or to escape the real. "The endeavor of the novelist, even by the lowest and most altruistic motives, is to tell untruths that will be diverting. . . . His primary endeavor must therefore be to divert not any possible reader, but himself." Hergesheimer usually preferred to combine illicit love with exotic settings; Cabell was not content until he had combined all of the possible extensions of romantic atmosphere with a steady and clever flouting of conventions. His hero, for the purpose of further exaggerating the effect, was usually the stoutest and soberest of burghers or the least attractive of leisure-class citizens. All of this to show beyond the shadow of a doubt that his imaginary world was as fake as his real one was dull.[3]

To the almost endless succession of "romances" beginning with the *Soul of Melicent* (1913) and including *Jurgen* (1919) and *The Silver Stallion* (1926) Cabell brought all of his empty cultivation of style and his haphazard erudition. *The Cream of the Jest* (1917) contains in one sense the disarming secret of his intention. Here, in the person of the novelist Felix Kennaston, are contained the two worlds in sharp enough contrast; and the intellectual basis of Kennaston's preference for the fantasy over the real is explained

---

[3] Mr. Cabell's attachment to Mencken, gained chiefly through the latter's exaggerated view of Cabell's merit, was perhaps less important than the fact that he belonged to another, a minor, development in modern fiction: beginning with the work of Edgar Saltus (1885–1921), which was deeply entangled in the *fin de siècle* views and the pseudo-symbolist language of the late 19th century, this tendency was taken up by James Huneker, whose novel *Painted Veils* (1920) was a running narrative commentary on its author's aesthetic and philosophic interests, and continued by Cabell and Carl Van Vechten. Van Vechten is perhaps the closest parallel to Cabell, in his mixture of topical satire and exotic themes, though he was capable of uninhibited and straightforward satirical treatments: of the bohemian world, of Hollywood, of the small Midwestern towns. All of these novelists are joined in several of their interests: their cultivation of an artificial style, fondness for a bohemian pose, and indebtedness to the varied intellectual interests of their times. The genuine and important use of symbolism and the literary techniques evident in this fiction, however, can best be seen in modern American poetry.

chiefly in slyly mocking comments upon his contemporary intellectual and artistic life. The clichés are there:

"Oh, well, all sensible people know, of course, that the trouble with prohibition is that it does not prohibit, and that woman's place is the home, not in the mire of politics."

The topical commentary, richly rewarding as it was to the social criticism of Mencken's world, added the spice of contemporary issues—the timidity and dullness of publishers and reviewers, the censorship, and the hard struggle that "beauty" might be beheld and appreciated.

In *Jurgen* all of the qualities of Cabell's mind were most sufficiently exercised. Here, in the mythical kingdom of Poictesme, the hero (who in real life is a pawnbroker with a shrewish wife) has his exotic and varied adventures. Jurgen is maneuvered through a succession of scenes, in settings devised in the highest style and with companions who are a mixture of Cabell's erudite background and facile imagination. In the end, after he has experienced the gracefully veiled voluptuous life with a variety of willing females, he returns to his wife, satisfied that Poictesme is not real and that he is, after all, not equal to the demands its temptations make upon him. The Poictesme of this novel is, in short, all of the things that are either shut out of or misunderstood by the world of Cabell's and Mencken's ministers, Legionnaires, and book reviewers. As if not satisfied that this point will be clear, Cabell has introduced his satire-within-a-fantasy through the opinions of the Philistine tumble-bugs:

"But in Philistia to make literature and to make trouble for yourself are synonyms," the tumble-bug explained. "I know, for already we of Philistia have been pestered by three of these makers of literature. Yes, there was Edgar, whom I starved and hunted until I was tired of it: then I chased him up a back alley one night, and knocked out those annoying brains of his. . . ."

There were also Walt and Mark; moreover, Jurgen is consigned to Hades in the end because he will not consent to pretend conformity to the philistine laws—though he would have become "Poet Laureate of Philistia" had he done so. The satire is never elsewhere so overtly parallel with what Mencken was enthusiastically applauding in contemporary journalism. But it continued sporadically to give the blessing of Poictesme to Mencken's labors in suburbia—the vexation, for example, of Grandfather Satan, over the demands made by the sinners from the world above, who never have a fire hot enough to equal the demands of their atoning conscience: "Their self-conceit is pitiful," say the over-worked devils; "but it is also a nuisance, because it prevents our getting any rest."

In *Jurgen* at least, we have another, and a precious, version of the results for fiction of the Mencken crusade against middle-class America. In its elaborate cultivation of a style that was admired excessively in its time but now seems vulgarly pretentious, in its apparently subtle but actually, superficial irony, and in its elaborate reliance upon myth and romance, the novel cannot conceal its final paucity of effect. Its popularity, like the success of other Cabell novels, can only be ascribed to the fact that its public was caught gratefully off guard, that they thought they had found a deeper meaning than was actually there, and that the principal attractiveness of the fantasy was erotic. The middle-class reader, like Lewis's Babbitt, dissatisfied with his Myra, was misled into thinking for the moment that Guenevere might take her place. The blandishments of Cabell's rhetoric were enough to keep the illusion momentarily alive, and they have also been sufficient to give *Jurgen,* the sole survivor of Cabell's early novels, a continuing reputation as a literary curiosity.

iv

". . . the author would like to say that never before did one try to keep his artistic conscience as pure as during the ten months put into doing it," Fitzgerald wrote, by way of introducing a reissue of *The Great Gatsby*. And, six months before his death, he wrote his daughter about that novel:

What little I've accomplished has been by the most laborious and uphill work, and I wish now I'd *never* relaxed or looked back—but said at the end of *The Great Gatsby:* "I've found my line—from now on this comes first. This is my immediate duty—without this I am nothing."

The Great Gatsby (1925) is F. Scott Fitzgerald's artistic center: to it all of the promise of his earlier fiction leads; to it the later work was always to be referred—by critics and by Fitzgerald himself, as the "line," the core of his achievement and art. Fitzgerald had succeeded in that novel against great odds; he had taken hold of materials that in their very richness might have defeated a score of more ambitious but less capable artists. He had, in short, brought into clear focus all of the preoccupations and experiences less capably treated in his earlier novels; and he never treated them so well again.

His career began with the publication of *This Side of Paradise* (1920). Two years before Scribner's finally accepted it for publication, Fitzgerald wrote to Edmund Wilson that "really if Scribner takes it I know I'll wake some morning and find that the debutantes have made me famous over night. I really believe that no one else could have written so searchingly the story of the youth of our generation." The confidence of youth spoke out here and predicted what did actually happen. From 1920 on, the generation he spoke of did support him for the rest of the decade; it "bore him up, flattered him and gave him more money than he had dreamed of, simply for telling people that he felt as they did, that something had to be done with all the nervous energy stored up and unexpended in the War."

The decade provided Fitzgerald with several opportunities—inded urged them upon him, who had become its most literate spokesman. There was the genuinely complex and vital problem of its wealth. So much had already been said in American fiction about the role of money in the history of American culture that only the most crucial moral change could have permitted fresh insights into it. That change was stimulated by the passing of the Eighteenth Amendment, which released a flood of controversial commentary upon postwar moralities and legalities. Fitzgerald was enormously interested in the social and moral influence of Prohibition's easy gold. Secondly, there was the question of the youth itself. A vast gulf yawned between the dissipations of Hemingway's Lady Brett and the self-important gestures of Gloria Gilbert of *The Beautiful and Damned* (1922); and it was one of Fitzgerald's more important tasks to describe the growth and the hardening of the girl generally labeled "flapper" in the 1920's; to both her and her young male escort—in or recently from Yale or Princeton—he directed much of his attention.

Perhaps his principal task and, in consequence, his chief merit, was to find a means for the accurate grasp of the entire surface world of the 1920's; that is, that world of Long Island and Manhattan which overflowed onto the Riviera and Paris. This was a crucial challenge; it was a problem for both his moral and his aesthetic conscience to solve. *This Side of Paradise* had done no more than prepare the way for it. The source of both Amory Blaine's money and his ideas was the earlier world of the 1890's and the two decades which followed. Amory Blaine's was a prewar mind and conscience, and he brought to his readers in 1920 what conclusions he could draw from a large and adolescent disillusionment with that world. As Amory's mind, so the novel's form: it was cluttered—its thoughts were ill-clad and ill-fed and indifferently sheltered. The thoughts of Fitzgerald's youthful hero were romantic in the best undergraduate meaning of that term. He rejected the pundits and the faiths of his fathers with the decisiveness and the amateur resolve of the adolescent.[4]

The novel was a beginning; or, rather, its success marked Fitzgerald's beginning. In the five years between it and *The Great Gatsby,* he could be seen (and literally) both enjoying his fame in the manner to which his readers were accustomed, and struggling honestly to make something more of his talent than an early success seemed to demand. *The Beautiful and Damned* showed some progress. Here were the parties and the frivolities of the two intervening years; there were also strong reminders of the pseudopoetic quality so abundantly present in the first novel. "He has the rare faculty of being able to experience romantic and ingenuous emotions and a half hour later regard them with satiric detachment," wrote John Peale Bishop, in a prepublication review of the book. "He has an amazing grasp of the superficialities of the men and women about him, but he has not

4 Another American novel which exploited many of the same themes as *This Side of Paradise* was Stephen Vincent Benét's *The Beginning of Wisdom* (1921). Among the novels which exploited the postwar interest in the "campus revolution in moralities" was Percy Marks's *The Plastic Age* (1924).

yet a profound understanding of their motives, either intellectual or passionate."

The time Fitzgerald spent in the writing of *The Great
Gatsby* was also devoted to a careful examination of his
weaknesses and a consolidation of whatever formal gains
he had made since the beginning. He had, as he said, not
only to find the most suitable approach to his materials but
also to justify these materials to himself: ". . . I had recently
been kidded half haywire by critics who felt that my material was such as to preclude all dealing with mature persons in a mature world. But, my God! it was my material,
and it was all I had to deal with." That material needed a
firm hand and a mature sense of formal structure; that it
did get both can easily be shown by a routine comparison
of the novel with others of its very popular type.

One of his happiest decisions was to present *The Great
Gatsby* through the mind and eye of a narrator only partially
committed to participating in and judging its world. Nick
Carraway is a key to the novel's considerable success. Carraway was not only interested in the fundamental decencies
("I am one of the few honest people that I have ever
known."); he was also firmly disposed to judge the people
around him with reference to them. It is important also that
Carraway should have come from the Midwest—both the
geographical and the moral Midwest. For Saint Paul had
been a point of moral return for Fitzgerald from the beginning of his adult career; the young men and women of many
of his short stories pass through Chicago—almost always
ignorant of it, whether it be Dreiser's Chicago or any other's
—on "the way back." Carraway had decided not to return
after World War I, because the Midwest "now seemed like
the ragged edge of the universe," but he brought his reserve
and his country suspicions to the bond business and to the

"small eyesore" of a house at West Egg. Everything that Carraway had was small-scale and unpretentious: his house "squeezed between two huge places that rented for twelve or fifteen thousand a season," his car, his cook who "muttered Finnish wisdom to herself" over the stove, his mind. The effect of all this upon the narrative is to reduce its materials to scale, and to make its frightening confusion and litter comprehensible and measurable.

It is in this way that we learn to know the almost fabulous Gatsby, with the full and honest advantage of Carraway's reductive and orderly judgment. What Edith Wharton had said of Gatsby is true[5]: Gatsby is not given in abundant and exhaustive detail, but continuously evoked and suggested, with a remarkable economy of effect which is a tribute to Carraway's tidy mind and Fitzgerald's sense of form. Gatsby needs just that sort of gradual and speculative construction; as his person and his mind slowly come into our attention, it is with Carraway's anxious concern over the truth of him that we receive him. What is at the beginning a grotesque and shabbily ostentatious world is thus continuously being reduced to the scale of observation entrusted to Fitzgerald's narrator.

Beyond that, and to enforce it, there is the symbolic organization given the novel's detail. Here again, the great progress made in the development of Fitzgerald's art is obvious. The Valley of Ashes which literally intervenes between Manhattan and the "two Eggs"; the symptomatically brooding eyes of Doctor T. J. Eckleburg, the valley's tutelary deity; the green light at the end of the Buchanan dock;

5 "My present quarrel with you is only this: that to make Gatsby really Great, you ought to have given us his early career (not from the cradle—but from his visit to the yacht, if not before) instead of a short résumé of it. That would have situated him, & made his final tragedy a tragedy instead of a 'fait divers' for the morning papers." Letter to Fitzgerald, June 8, 1925; in *The Crack-up*, p. 309.

the El Greco scene near the close of the novel; a Midwest-erner's self-consciously distorted image of his despair over the amoral callousness of the world of Gatsby's parties—these are a major symbolic means of bringing chaos within the scope of an ordered view. They might have seemed only factitiously effective were it not that they are accompanied throughout by a most skillful power of evocation. Through it a few details are made to serve a large purpose—as in this description of the apartment where Tom Buchanan keeps his mistress on their trips to New York. In its portrayal of vulgar and crowded taste reside implications of the violence to come:

The apartment was on the top floor—a small living-room, a small dining-room, a small bedroom, and a bath. The living-room was crowded to the doors with a set of tapestried furniture entirely too large for it, so that to move about was to stumble continually over scenes of ladies swinging in the gardens of Ver-sailles. The only picture was an over-enlarged photograph, ap-parently a hen sitting on a blurred rock. Looked at from a dis-tance, however, the hen resolved itself into a bonnet, and the countenance of a stout old lady beamed down into the room. Several old copies of *Town Tattle* lay on the table together with a copy of *Simon Called Peter,* and some of the small scandal magazines of Broadway.

Similarly, in sharp, brief images, Fitzgerald achieves the *multum in parvo* effect of great fictional art; Wolfsheim "began to eat with ferocious delicacy;" the Buchanans "drifted here and there unrestfully wherever people played polo and were rich together;" Gatsby's cream-colored car was "bright with nickel, swollen here and there in its mon-strous length with triumphant hat-boxes and supper-boxes and tool-boxes, and terraced with a labyrinth of wind-shields that mirrored a dozen suns;" the grateful surprise of "Owl-Eyes" in Gatsby's library over the fact that the books were real served to increase his admiration for his host: "The fella's a regular Belasco. It's a triumph. What thoroughness! What realism! Knew when to stop, too—didn't cut the pages. . . ."

As we are led to Gatsby through the mind and moral sense of Carraway, so we are asked to view his death as Carraway has viewed it. The world of Gatsby's West Egg estate has collapsed as soon as there is any risk of its being challenged by the real world. After Gatsby's death, Wolfsheim will not go near him; Klipspringer, "the boarder," calls up, but only to claim his tennis shoes; Gatsby's business associates hang up with a "sharp click" when they learn what has happened; and only Owl-Eyes is there to join the small funeral procession. Nick Carraway is left, not only to see to Gatsby's decent burial but to make something of his strange story. Coming back for one last time, before his return to "the bored, sprawling, swollen towns beyond the Ohio," he takes up the romantic illusion where Gatsby's death has left it, and tries to bring away from West Egg a final reconstruction of its meaning. He has not only fully accepted Gatsby as the only person of his New York experience who is secure in his judgment; he has gone beyond that, to associate Gatsby with American tradition: the Dutch sailors' eyes who had first seen Long Island as "a fresh, green breast of the new world" are its beginning; the mansion of James J. Hill is a symbol of its gross opportunity; the figure of Dan Cody, whose magic influence has changed drab James Gatz into Jay Gatsby, represents the beginning of decadence; and Gatsby himself, to look at him through Carraway's eyes, is a tragic victim of its final exhaustion: "He did not know that [his dream] was already behind him, somewhere back in that vast obscurity beyond the city, where the dark fields of the republic rolled on under the night."

After *The Great Gatsby,* Fitzgerald's next great opportunity was to study the world of America's more fashionable expatriates: in sickness at Zurich, and in health at the Riviera. This was an opportunity equally challenging, and Fitzgerald worked at it on the scene in Europe. There were several attempts to bring the immense theme within manageable limits. At one time he had thought of centering the entire narrative upon a Hollywood character come to Europe and there committed to matricide; he changed that conception, fortunately, but kept its idea of Hollywood on vacation. To the detailed portrayal of Americans rich and idle in Europe he brought another theme, equally suggestive and potentially important. The end-result of all of these beginnings was the novel, *Tender Is the Night* (1934). But, while *The Great Gatsby* is brilliantly restrained in its use of material, this novel is huge and sprawling. Its first section is viewed through the eyes of Rosemary Hoyt, who sees the Divers and their friends naïvely, with the fresh wonder of Hollywood's screen star out for the first time to check the world against her celluloid vision of it. But this point of view, as a sufficient means in itself, is obviously not what Fitzgerald wants; and we find him veering awkwardly away from it, at times toward the Divers' point of view, at times toward omniscience. And we have such embarrassing reminders of his failure to manage as "To resume Rosemary's point of view it should be said that . . ." It is obvious from the beginning that Rosemary Hoyt is a most unsuccessful entrance to the world of Dick and Nicole Diver, and it is on their terms that the rest of the novel is written.

That story involves the use of a theme that American novelists had been fumbling with since the end of World War I: the problem of the psychoanalytic situation—in this case, the problem in a doctor-patient relationship. Of *Tender Is the Night* it can at least be said that the relationship is handled with honesty, often with knowledge, and occasionally with skill. But it is not so much the mechanics of the "science" as these are brought to bear upon the narrative that makes the novel worth considering. Fitzgerald has tried to link the fullest implication of the clinic and sanitarium to the significance of the expatriate world. Wherever he does that, it is in terms of a minor note in the whole clamorous discord: the failure of aspiration and ambition. Diver's is the major failure; but, on other levels of the narrative there are minor failures: Abe North's; the failure ironically suggested in McKisco's success as a derivative novelist; the pathos of Campion the homosexual; and, finally, the genuinely acute insight into what rests beneath the surface of "Baby" Warren's imperious smugness and Rosemary's quick transition from innocence to hardness of character.

Tender Is the Night is not a successful novel. It shows, on the one hand, the consequences of a too hasty composition; on the other, the results of a prolonged but fumbling concern over form. Omniscience, here assumed (when we can be sure that it *is* assumed) with a half-hearted and embarrassed will, fails its purpose as thoroughly as Carraway's point of view had succeeded.

That Fitzgerald was aware of the failure is indicated in his attempt to salvage the method of *The Great Gatsby* in the novel he left unfinished at his death. As we see it in the version Edmund Wilson has edited, *The Last Tycoon* (published in 1941) has returned to the modified first-person point of view—in this case, the daughter of a Hollywood producer, Cecilia Brady. While his tendency had been, in *The Great Gatsby,* toward economy, precision, and re-

straint, here as in *Tender Is the Night* he is defeated by
the richness and complexity of his theme, which the rather
weakly delineated sensibility of Miss Brady is scarcely
equipped to cope with. Though Nathanael West's *Day of
the Locust* (1939) has its own reasons for failure, it is much
more successful in isolated scenes and in sharpness of focus
than Fitzgerald's fictional view of Hollywood.

Fitzgerald's novels have a significant place in modern
American fiction, and this not only because, like Hemingway, he worked consciously toward the perfection of his art.
He has proved, in those places where it did succeed, that it
was possible to create an acceptable order out of materials
that proved very difficult to his contemporaries. He had
neither the security of background nor the balance of subject that it was the good fortune of James and Wharton to
have. Yet he came very close to providing the American
1920's their full measure of what he himself called "truth
or rather the *equivalent* of the truth, the attempt at honesty
of imagination." It is undeniably true that he brought no
interpretation of his own to bear upon this record of his
imagination. That he was neither trained for, nor interested
in, the life of the mind he admits again and again in his letters and notebooks. And William Troy's objection to the
lack must be accepted as true:

Perhaps it is not well for the novelist to encumber himself with
too much knowledge, although one cannot help recalling the
vast cultural apparatus of a Tolstoy or a Joyce, or the dialecti-
cal intrepidity of a Dostoevsky or a Mann. And recalling these
Europeans, none of whom foundered on the way, one wonders
whether a certain coyness toward the things of the mind is not
one reason for the lack of development in most American writers.
Art is not intellect; but without intellect art is not likely to
emerge beyond the plane of perpetual immaturity.

Fitzgerald did succeed in avoiding the pitfall of a too easy ideological support for fiction, a trap most of his contemporaries of the 1930's were caught in (many of them went so far as to set the trap themselves). Except for the obviously adolescent appeals in his first two novels to classroom and dormitory storehouses of information and ideas, he was successful beyond all of his contemporaries in keeping his work free of the pretentious intellectual faking that has handicapped so much of American fiction since Norris and Dreiser. Yet, as his novels derive their greatest merit from his intimate feeling for the exact idiom of the present, so they possess the limitations of a mind unable to go beyond that present—frequently unable to stand outside it. He was often quite literally immersed in the present, and had only an imperfectly trained talent for viewing that present objectively and without sentimentality. The really great contribution he has made to the fiction record of that present ought not to be ignored, however. If he lacked what Farrell calls Dreiser's sense of social structures, he was also happily free of Dreiser's disastrous failure of taste. Gatsby therefore very frequently succeeds where Cowperwood fails, as an imaginative figuration of a fact in America's cultural history. We may well conclude, therefore, that what Arthur Mizener calls Fitzgerald's "happy incapacity for subduing his imagination to any system of abstract categories" left him free to make the most of a real if limited talent.

6

VIOLENCE AND RHETORIC IN THE 1930's

i

OF THE scores of essays and books which appeared in the 1930's in defense and explanation of the leftist imperative in the arts, perhaps Ralph Fox's *The Novel and the People* (1937) is most relevant to our purpose. Written by a British leftist who died fighting in Spain in the year of its publication, this book attempts to survey the English novel and, primarily, to attach definitive judgments to the twentieth-century novel. It is heavily weighted with the near-clichés and half-clichés of leftist criticism, though it misses by some lengths the raw, literal dogmatism of much contemporary American discussion of the novel. Much of the great work in the history of the English novel, says Fox, is the story of the struggle against a capitalist society or of one or another evasion of that struggle. So he speaks of Fielding's living in a "brutal world, the world of conquering capitalism," of Jane Austen's "world of sheltered gentility;" he says that he regards the three greatest books of the nineteenth century (*Wuthering Heights, Jude the Obscure,* and *The Way of All Flesh*) as "the manifestoes of English genius that a full human life in a capitalist society was impossible of attainment." As for the contemporary novel, Fox regrets chiefly that it has denied the existence of the principle of a hero and that its authors had no real understanding of the working man. The central task of the modern novelist is, therefore, to "create . . . the hero of our times, and in this way to become, as Stalin has phrased it, 'an engineer of the human soul.' " Only the revolutionary novelist is equipped for this task; he is working in a new literature "free from the anarchist individualism of the bourgeoisie in its period of decay." He alone is able "to create the hero of our times, the complete picture of modern life, because only he is able to perceive the truth of that life."

What follows in Mr. Fox's book is especially relevant to the leftist fiction of the 1930's. The crucial difference, he says, between the writers of that decade and those of the 1920's lies in the attitude toward the laboring class. Hemingway had created a "brutal, but simple and inarticulate working man." Huxley's *Brave New World* (1932) and Rice's play, *The Adding Machine* (1923) were two of many examples in literature which portrayed "the mechanical man," brutalized and stupefied by the machine. But man fights mechanization all the way, says Fox; he tries not to escape but to use it.

All of these remarks were, of course, paralleled with only slight variation in America by Granville Hicks, Joseph Freeman, and Michael Gold, in *The New Masses, Partisan*

Review, Dynamo, The Anvil, and a score of other magazines. Along with the development of an American leftist
criticism came the phenomenon of the proletarian novel.
Dozens of these appeared in the decade, and their authors
rode along comfortably in a temporary state of ideological
prosperity. There were variations of talent and degrees of
excellence, but in the decade a novel could be praised primarily for its author's sincerity of purpose and the proletarian nature of his background, and the judgment might
well set aside all other views of his work. There was a formula of proletarian fiction which held in one crude way or
another to the need for Marxist demonstration. First, it
ought to be a novel of action—which meant that it usually
contained much action and that the pace was relatively fast;
as for the reader, he was supposed to be stimulated, if not to
action, at least to a very active sympathy with the patently
"right cause" about which the fiction left no doubt. Second,
in this kind of novel thought was subordinated to the action
as it was seen preparing and occurring. The intellectual development of the characters was both logically simple and
ideologically determined. Part of the strategy often used
was to begin in a state of doubt or fear, which the crystal
clear action that subsequently occurred served to dissipate.
Third, there was a measure of documentation in every one
of these novels, and some of them were nothing but documentation. Never in the history of American fiction were
facts of the American scene so abundantly supplied or so
frequently reiterated. This aspect of the fiction was traceable partly to the journalistic tradition from which it took
its being; but the principal reason for it was the driving
need for documentary realism—an urgent and feverishly
earnest reliance upon the "dogma of induction."

As for the novel's hero, there were relatively few variations upon a single-minded theme: the hero must carry the burden of ideological conviction. In a genuine sense, the masses were the hero, but its general conviction must be articulated and individualized in one member or a few. The hero might begin as an uneducated worker; or he might actually be a reactionary, a "scab." However he begins, he is soon informed, and his mind set right, by both event and doctrinal persuasion. The dialogue, therefore, when it did not follow the earnest effort of these novelists to secure a regional accuracy of dialect, took the form of a dialectic catechism. The answers were all there, and the experienced reader did not have to look for them in the back of the book. Most of all, however, the dialogue was a part of the ideological preparation for an interpretation of coming events, or an ideological summary of the meaning of events recently past.

The proletarian novel took manifest advantage of all of the advances made in fictional style in the preceding decade. Through birth, background, and training, the novelist was inclined to adopt a modified version of Hemingway's simplicity; seldom did this simplicity go beneath the surface of reportage; there was no need for any refinement of style since the intellectual purpose served by it had long since been decided upon. Far from reaching honestly toward a definition of character, this style proved simply useful and served to set aside questions of craft and discipline. In addition, proletarian novelists had access, in their own view of contemporary events, to an obvious and crude irony. It was a social irony, the natural result of an ironic difference between the "haves" and the "have-nots" (the have-littles were only infrequently featured). This was a ready-made, utilitarian irony; its uses were early formularized and reiterated *ad nauseam*.

All of this refers, of course, to the "garden run" of proletarian novelists, to those who actually wrote according to a formula and who possessed little or no talent for either modifying or individualizing. These novelists produced several kinds of leftist document: there were, for one, the novels of factory life, in which the dangers of mechanization were discussed and one or another formula for fighting them suggested: Edwin Seaver's *The Company* (1930); William Wister Haines's *Slim* (1934), Albert Maltz's *The Underground Stream* (1940). A variant of this type is the melodramatic strike novel, in which the mechanics and dynamics of the strike contribute the motivating and activating power: Mary Heaton Vorse's *Strike!* (1930); William Rollins, Jr.'s *The Shadow Before* (1934); Clara Weatherwax's *Marching! Marching!* (1935). The facts of unemployment, of desperate poverty, of the depression voyages of the underprivileged in search of bare subsistence, were the sum and substance of many proletarian documents: Edward Newhouse's *You Can't Sleep Here* (1934); Jack Conroy's *The Disinherited* (1933); Robert Cantwell's *The Land of Plenty* (1931); Edward Dahlberg's *Bottom Dogs* (1930). Closely allied in form and subject were the novels of city slums, tenements, and streets: Michael Gold's *Jews Without Money* (1930); Nelson Algren's *Somebody in Boots* (1935). Occasionally, these novelists provided the leftist family saga to compete with the bulky family romances which had been staple best-sellers for decades; such a one was Josephine Herbst's trilogy which carried the history of a middle-class family from the years immediately following the Civil War to the 1930's: *Pity Is Not Enough* (1933); *The Executioner Waits* (1934); *Rope of Gold* (1938). And we have at least one novel which portrayed with an undoctrinal subtlety the lonely role of the leftist intellectual in the city, Tess Slesinger's *The Unpossessed* (1934).

If anything can be said by way of generalizing about these novels, it is that they enjoyed the reputation provided them by a moment in history, but that, having thus bargained for their popularity, they were soon forgotten when that moment passed. They relied upon the speciously real and the dogmatically convincing for their effect; but only a very few of their authors survived the passing of that kind of reality and conviction.[1] Several effects may be noticed, however, for the history of fiction in the next decade. For one thing, the interest in this fiction in the 1930's was at least partly induced by its scenes of violence. This interest in violence has survived the occasion more than any other thing. As a stimulus to the reading of fiction it had, of course, antedated the 1930's, but not a few of the proletarian novelists were skilled in the description of sudden action, mass movement, clashes with the police, and indiscriminate clubbing and killing. No interest has been more thoroughly exploited than this in the fiction of the last ten years. The break from the useful association of violence with ideology is seen in the stresses and strains of Richard Wright's best-seller *Native Son* (1940). Wright's purpose was sincerely enough a part of the general leftist point of view; but, as Alfred Kazin has said, "his own indignation and the sickness of the age combined to make him dependent on violence and shock, to astonish the reader by torrential scenes of cruelty, hunger, rape, murder, and flight and then enlighten him by crude Stalinist homilies." The interest in *Native Son* was at least equally divided between the violence itself and Wright's strenuously earnest use of its social implications.

---

[1] Among the few novelists whose work merited survival of the leftist ideological "defeat" was Meyer Levin, two of whose novels, *The Old Bunch* (1937) and *Citizens* (1940) were considerably above the average of their kind.

Another result for the subsequent history of our fiction is perhaps very far from the intention of leftist novelists. They had courageously documented the human and physical wastes of American life, confident in the semi-Marxist premise from which their records proceeded. That premise removed or discredited and the heroics which depended upon it thus nullified, the naturalist novel subsequently developed in a way designed simply to portray the world itself. Therefore, we have novels which certainly describe more skillfully the world of Skid Row, but do it without a dogmatic purpose. Nelson Algren's *The Man with the Golden Arm* (1950), and, at least in part, Willard Motley's *Knock on Any Door* (1947) and Ira Wolfert's *Tucker's People* (1943) are such stories of the underground man.

ii

The three novelists of the left or near-left whose work lifts them above the dead level of the proletarian formula novel are John Dos Passos, James T. Farrell, and John Steinbeck. Dos Passos' major work is of course the massive trilogy *U.S.A.* (*The Forty-Second Parallel*, 1930; *Nineteen-Nineteen*, 1932; and *The Big Money*, 1936). He had earlier, in *Manhattan Transfer* (1925), experimented with what critics have since called the "collectivist novel," satisfied there with the Manhattan setting alone. In *U.S.A.* he expanded the physical and social range of his setting, introduced several new structural devices and reduced the importance of any one character in the interests of giving a dead-level equality of attention to all of them. Jimmy Herf of *Manhattan Transfer*, survivor of Dos Passos' still earlier fiction, is the sensitively honest soul in an alien world who dramatically announces his incompatibility with that world. He is also a hint of what in Dos Passos' writing after *U.S.A.* became a primary concern; in his traditional origins (one of his ancestors had died in the Revolutionary War) he points to Dos Passos' own pride in the American tradition described in *The Ground We Stand On* (1941); in his refusal to take advantage of his chances in the business world, he performs the act of renunciation so remote from the wills of most of *U.S.A.'s* people; in his solitary assertion of the precious values of individualism, he is the 1920's version of Dos Passos' later hero, Glenn Spotswood of *Adventures of a Young Man* (1939).

Dos Passos' work had almost regularly dwelt upon a major preoccupation: the defeat of individualism in the modern world. In its aesthetic forms this individualism was that of the sensitive young man (the Martin Howe of *One Man's Initiation,* John Andrews of *Three Soldiers*). More and more, as we proceed from novel to novel, this young man becomes clearly and poignantly aware of his being ineffectual and out of place. He is quite indignant in his earlier incarnations; as the emphasis shifts in Dos Passos' fiction, from the sensitive young man as victim to the social configurations of *Manhattan Transfer* and *U.S.A.,* his hero all but disappears from the scene. If *U.S.A.* has a character reminiscent of him, it is the author-artist of the "Camera Eye," who suffers all and sees all but is helpless to change whatever he sees. Society has closed in upon him. *U.S.A.* is, therefore, a massive document of twentieth-century American society, a condemned society impulsively, repetitiously working out its dismal sentence. Dos Passos had abandoned his earlier idea of an isolated victim and turned to the all-inclusive task of documenting both agent and victim of America's social and economic drives.

U.S.A. is a fictional history of America in the first three decades of our century. Both time and space are vitally important to this history, and it is to the mass quality of these decades that the trilogy addresses itself. *The Forty-Second Parallel* is a portrayal of its youth: here there are energy and promise, the beginnings of industrial greatness and business strategy; there is youth also in the individualism of "Mac," the IWW vagabond (who contrasts with the generally unflattering portraits of Communist organizers in the later volumes) and in the adolescent gestures of the other characters. It is a youth, however, that carries within it, not the promise of successful independence but the certainty of eventual surrender to the social and economic drives even here gathering strength. *Nineteen-Nineteen* is a record of the war, of the inevitable triumph of its predominating concerns over whatever native and individual strength the characters of the first novel had seemed to have. The war itself is a preparation for the documentation of the boom years in *The Big Money*. This last novel presents a culmination of all of the developments so exhaustively detailed in the first two novels. If anything, the figure of Charley Anderson detaches itself from the prison of documentation; in his reckless and mad drive toward wealth and finally to death, his role is a symbolic underscoring of all of the drives which are here dramatically culminated.

If *U.S.A.* has within it a purpose, it is not to point readily or easily to solutions or to point up doctrinal strategies. The leftists are as dismally treated as the professional exploiters; the evidence, if anything, points to their being ridiculous and unhappy creatures. And whatever gratification one may derive from the biographies of such men as Debs, La Follette and John Reed—portrayed as selfless and dedicated spirits—is obtained in the face of the recognition that they too are largely ineffectual. To this massive document of corruption and materialistic obsession, Dos Passos brings the timid observation and the self-defeating despair of the Camera Eye's consciousness. It is both a way of underscoring the gross triumph of the world of *U.S.A.* and of pointing up the inadequacy of the Camera Eye's protesting insight. For *U.S.A.* is not a tragedy so much as it is a holocaust; and it is a holocaust because, however effective its narrative style is, its success leads mainly to a deadening, automaton equality of motive and action. The manner is that of the surface reporter at his most brilliant. Dos Passos is unequalled in his talent for manipulating social and economic history in fictional forms; the details are selected with an almost uncannily acute perception of their pertinence; the exactly right surface record, from the newsreels and the tabloids, is always at hand; the narratives achieve a pace and a surface conviction of detail that are ideally suited to the final dramatic impact of the culminating scenes of *The Big Money*.

There is an awful inevitability in all this. Yet no one character seems to have escaped either its documentary drive or its essential superficiality. Any single scene in the trilogy suffers from the consequences of the method and purpose which dominate the whole. In achieving this purpose, individual effects must be sacrificed; or, rather, their effectiveness stops at the boundary of demonstration. The limitations of the following passage are not unlike those found in any comparable section of the trilogy. They are limitations of insight, evidences of an all-pervading and deliberate shallowness in the characterization.

Dick had an exam to repeat in Geometry which he'd flunked in the spring and one in Advanced Latin that he was taking for extra credits, so he went up to Cambridge a week before college

opened. He sent his trunk and suitcase out by the transfer company from the South Station and went out on the subway. He
had on a new grey suit and a new grey felt hat and was afraid
of losing the certified cheque he had in his pocket for deposit
in the Cambridge bank. The glimpse of redbrick Boston and the
state house with its gold dome beyond the slatecolored Charles
as the train came out into the air to cross the bridge looked like
the places in foreign countries he and Hilda had talked about
going to. Kendall Square . . . Central Square . . . Harvard Square.
The train didn't go any further; he had to get out. Something
about the sign on the turnstile *Out to the College Yard* sent a
chill down his spine. He hadn't been in Cambridge two hours
before he discovered that his felt hat ought to have been brown
and old instead of new and that getting a room in the Yard had
been a grave mistake for a freshman.

The details go no deeper and say no more, anywhere else,
about the inner life of his characters; instead there is a sense
of the need to rush on from one to another, giving on the
way a wholly factual, surface record of men and women in
motion and conflict but not in thought or reflection. Yet
there are no lapses of taste, no violations of a fictional decorum previously established. The tone of the three novels
is remarkably consistent throughout. It is the tone of the
passage quoted above—never more pretentious or less superficial. If there are ranges of emotional volume, degrees of
emotional intensity with the narrative itself, these are to be
found in the "Camera Eye," where indignation and despair
provide the only tonal commentary upon the narrative; and
in the strategy of the whole, the "Camera Eye" is itself objectively placed and reacts not at all upon its final effect as
the cries of young Howe and young Andrews, or the criticisms of Jimmy Herf, do upon theirs. As Kazin has said,
"for Dos Passos there is nothing else, save the integrity of the
camera eye that must see this truth and report it, the integ-

rity and sanctity of the individual locked up in the machine world of modern society."

iii

If the quiet and sustained world of Edith Wharton's fiction seemed inappropriate to the world of Dos Passos, it was entirely excluded from Farrell's. Here, in the Chicago of Studs Lonigan, Danny O'Neill, and Gas House McGinty, there was not only no attempt to find the sophistication and subtlety of an earlier decorum; there was absolutely no experience of it. *Young Lonigan* (1932), *The Young Manhood of Studs Lonigan* (1934), and *Judgment Day* (1935)—the novels of the Studs Lonigan trilogy were written in the self-effacing and reductive idiom of Studs himself. Herein are the demands of a point of view reduced to their lowest level; the style had not only to be equal to the subject, it had literally to *be* the subject. The consciousness was that of the spiritually impoverished lower middle class of a section of Chicago which is slowly deteriorating under social and economic pressures. It is true that Farrell, especially in the second of these novels, echoed and imitated the experiments of his more daring contemporaries, noticeably Joyce and Dos Passos; and in *Gas House McGinty* (1933) he very deliberately, and with a measure of success, tried to transport the mind of Leopold Bloom from Dublin to Chicago. Aside from these experimental excursions, Farrell relied upon a literal rendering of his subject, at once subjective in its following of point of view and objective in its freedom from sentimentality of record.

In a revealing confession, Farrell described in 1938 "How *Studs Lonigan* Was Written." He had been encouraged by two University of Chicago professors, James Weber Linn

and Robert Morss Lovett, to explore the possibilities suggested by a short story, "Studs." It was a problem of social
and cultural causation—the story of Studs's progress to the
funeral described in the short story. "I saw in the character
of Studs Lonigan a number of tendencies at work in a section of American life which I happened to know because it
had been part of my own education in living." These "tendencies," Farrell explains, had to do with the Irish-Catholic
world of a section of Chicago. It was not a slum neighbor-
hood; nor were the stages in Studs's decline designed to
illustrate an economic thesis. "The social milieu in which
he lived and was educated was one of spiritual poverty," in
short, the effect of a failure of moral sanctions rather than
of economic dislocation. "The important institutions in the
education of Studs Lonigan were the home and the family,
the church, the school, and the playground. These institutions broke down and did not serve their desired function.
The streets become a potent educative factor in the boy's
life. In time, the pool room becomes an important institu-
tion in his life."

In describing what happens as a result of this failure, Farrell tries very hard to show Studs Lonigan in the process
of maturing under the grim and dismal circumstances it
has been his misfortune to live in. He is capable of decision, makes his own choices; but in the limitations of these
choices, his life is in a sense determined. We are to assume
that his preference for the street is arrived at consciously
and that his progress in dissipation is made with full realization of its moral and physical effects. The religious vision
of evil which is so graphically given him by Father Gil-
hooley does serve to give him pause, and certainly causes
in him the retrospective agonies of conscience he frequently
suffers. His is also a "romantic soul," who sees in the figure

of Lucy Scanlan possibilities of another kind of life, but that life is as unreal in its way as the way to the priesthood which his mother vainly hopes he will take. But *Studs Lonigan* is not *Maggie;* the Chicago of Indiana Avenue is not Crane's Bowery. For all the reductive vulgarity of gang speech and behavior, there is a conscious effort to reach beyond this world for a mode of life that will triumph over its necessity and renounce the temptation to perpetuate its grim history. Danny O'Neill, the "punk" of *Studs Lonigan,* the "goof" of *Gas House McGinty,* becomes the hero of the tetralogy devoted to his quite self-sufficient career. This is a triumph over environment which is gained only by means of his educating himself out of the streets, eventually to use them as the very material of his success. Danny O'Neill-Bernard Clare-James Farrell succeeds where Studs fails because he acquires a reputation for honest and earnest writing; while Studs is a victim of the environment, O'Neill becomes the naturalist hero who expropriates and exploits the naturalist world in his writings. He is the scholar, the artist, the novelist of Studs, looking back from Studs's funeral to Studs's Chicago and making capital of all of it. There is a sense of earnest self-importance which qualifies all of the portrayal of Danny O'Neill; it is a self-conscious and embarrassed portrait of the man who, while in Studs's world, is getting ready to survey and judge it.

No one has so thoroughly and so doggedly described a single area of American society as we find in the seven novels of Studs Lonigan and Danny O'Neill. The constant reiteration of the trivial and the vulgar, the thoroughly naturalistic view of the ugly and terrifying lives of these people, have a cumulative effect which is chiefly the result of Farrell's conscientious fidelity to the subject's idiom. The style, therefore, is consistently a documentary record of this world from the point of view of those who live in it and share its limitations—who in a real sense, *make* its limitations. An important part of the effect, therefore, lies in the conscientious vulgarity, profanity, and obscenity of the language—as well as the earnest inelegance of the narrative's loose and repetitive structure. There is a quality of tone, however, which enables us to see Farrell's characters more clearly (that is, to understand the tone of their feeling) than we can ever do in the case of Dos Passos' novels. The passage which follows, for example, while not so spectacular as, say, the wild New Year's Eve scenes of *The Young Manhood of Studs Lonigan,* does suggest quite well the moderate effectiveness of Farrell's style:

The old man said that smoking stunted a boy's growth, ruined his health, disrupted his moral sense, and was against . . . nature. He lit a long stogy. Frances said smoking was nasty, and Studs said nobody asked her for her two cents. Mrs. Lonigan said that it might give him TB. Studs kept wishing they would can the sermon. He asked them to cut it out, and he was reminded of the commandment to honor thy father and thy mother. He said he had some rights. The blah went back and forth.

Farrell did not consistently succeed in maintaining this virtue of literal integrity. Quite often his work reveals serious lapses in taste. In fact, he is quite like Dreiser in the sin that both commit when they are tempted to indulge in the "high style." This failure is especially noticeable in the novels written after the Lonigan and O'Neill series—in *Ellen Rogers* (1941), for example, from which this passage can be used as indicative:

"The essential characteristic of the romantic is that he seeks the Unattainable along the highways and byways of the world. He is always traveling toward the mirage on the far horizon. He is embarked on an endless quest, and for what? The most important object of desire in life. The beauty of the will-o'-the-wisp. But he is doomed never to find that." He paused before changing to a lighter tone. "But, Sweet, you and I have come very close to finding the Unattainable."

Of course, this is in character; it is what Ed Lanson and not what Farrell says. But it is a part of what Farrell is seriously trying to say in the novel, and the crude mechanics of plot only serve to emphasize his inability to represent a world even slightly more complex than that of Studs Lonigan and Danny O'Neill.

iv

Writing to Covici-Friede, his publishers, about the ideological tactics of *In Dubious Battle* (1936), Steinbeck said, "My information for this book came mostly from Irish and Italian Communists whose training was in the field, not in the drawing-room. They don't believe in ideologies and ideal tactics. They do what they can under the circumstances." This is the kind of orientation to which Steinbeck addressed himself throughout the 1930's, the period of his best-known novels. His remarkable, almost uncanny ability to meet the intellectual and emotional needs of a depression-trained reading public contrasts vividly with the work of those novelists who, with almost missionary zeal, were trying to influence the public mind. He was "ideologically inadequate," in the view of the New York leftist intellectual. *In Dubious Battle* was not in line with "orthodox party principles." That is probably what saved it from being just another strike novel, although just what orthodox party principles were was an unanswerable critical question. Steinbeck, in this story of a fruit-pickers' strike in Torgas Valley, had tried to see the strike as the material of a novel. In its boldly simple outlines, he was able to exploit in full measure the dramatic and intellectual possibilities of this depression-sponsored social fact. Steinbeck had supposed that the strike involved several matters: a mass of men who, though pliable and maneuverable, did have a certain reserve of unpredictable reactions; a hard, practical party organizer, who was a genius at adjusting and exploiting the day-by-day behavior of such a group; a neophyte, whose education in strike tactics and party spirit should take place rapidly and with melodramatic effect; finally, an impartial observer, to take the place of the ideological mouthpiece usually found in strike novels. This last must be a scientist interested in being active during the strike for what he called "objective reasons," but practically necessary to the strike as well.

All of these he provided; and the major strategy was to develop the activist and emotive essentials of the strike in terms of them all. The men have first to be unified, and it is here that the genius of Mac, the party organizer, is revealed; they have to be held in line as well, and in the course of their being held firm, the dramatics of psychological opportunism are exploited. Nowhere else are the facts of violence and death so skillfully interwoven with the rest of the design of the strike novel. The facts of "ideological death" have become more and more important in modern fiction; eventually they have come to serve a novelistic view of the modern world quite thoroughly dissociated from leftist strategies as such. The deaths of Joy and Jim in *In Dubious Battle* are a starkly simple literary examination of this kind of strategic sacrifice. In the nature of their self-effacement they lead to Malraux's cyanide capsules in *Man's*

Fate,[2] and ultimately to the purely mechanical deaths of the aviators of Randall Jarrell's poetry.

The major development of this novel's strike theme is to be found in the several discussions among the three men who view it wholly or partly from an intellectual point of view. Doc Burton is of course almost wholly committed to that point of view. He "wants to see," he explains; he wants to examine group man as a biological organism. It is a lonely life, this task of looking at group man objectively, resisting the temptation to share in its passionate outbursts of strong emotion, for fear of losing the priceless weapon of the objective view. "I'm awfully lonely. I'm working all alone, towards nothing. There's some compensation for you people. I only hear heartbeats through a stethoscope. You hear them in the air."

In the balanced opposition of intellect and purpose of these three men lies the value of this novel as a useful literary expression of the strike theme. It was this pattern of ideological checks and balances which surprised most critics who had in this decade expected such facts as a strike produces to yield to a single interpretation, or at least a sustained complex of views. Steinbeck was not to repeat this accomplishment in his fiction, for taken as a whole, his novels reveal the deficiencies of a homespun philosophy, in which the suggestions made are vitiated and confused by a "hausfrau sentimentality" and a naïve mysticism.

The two principal influences upon this point of view are the land itself—it is a special kind of land, a California valley—and the biologist's laboratory. The land itself served as a test of persons; it helped to classify people: those who loved the land with what sometimes amounted to pagan worship, and those who exploited it. This is a division not

2 André Malraux, *La Condition Humaine* (1933).

too uncommon in modern American fiction, but it is a very significant one for Steinbeck's. It led, in short, to the kind of oversimplification of issues (when issues had finally forced themselves upon Steinbeck's attention) which is in part sentimentality and in part a basic democratic earnestness and sincerity. Were it not for Steinbeck's amateurish interest in the biologist's laboratory, it might have led simply to still another American novelist in the Whitman-Sandberg literary tradition. Steinbeck's curiosity about the behavior of small animals substantially reduced the intellectual content of his novels as it reduced the emotional plane on which his tragedies occur. This is a fact of his novels that Edmund Wilson has very shrewdly observed:

The chief subject of Mr. Steinbeck's fiction has been thus not those aspects of humanity in which it is most thoughtful, imaginative, constructive, nor even those aspects of animals that seem most attractive to humans, but rather the processes of life itself. In the natural course of nature, living organisms are continually being destroyed, and among the principal things that destroy them are the predatory appetite and the competitive instinct that are necessary for the very survival of eating and breeding creatures.

A determining factor in the judgment of Steinbeck's fiction is the way in which this view, if sentimentally indulged, acts to confuse whatever intellectual strategy he uses with his material. For, though Steinbeck has the curiosity of his scientists, he has neither the need nor the desire for their disciplines. The curiosity is thus essentially self-indulgent; it betrays many of his fictional plans and reduces others to the level where he asks us not only to view the human as animal nature but to *believe* in him as such. The idiots of Steinbeck's fiction are a case in point; there is no attempt to make us realize their idiocy in the perspective of a larger fictional strategy; instead we are reduced to a comparable subrational level of appreciation and sympathy. This attitude leads to the fundamental intellectual weakness of Steinbeck's novels. He is unable to give us a convincing definition of his people because, having once reduced the *scale* of definition to their animal nature, he has subsequently shifted his ground of interpretation and with a desperate earnestness grasped at the most superficial but convenient ideational strategy available to him in the 1930's.

For a rather large part of the 1930's mind "the land" served symbolically as an admonitory and argumentative premise. The land, and the people who modestly, that is, "democratically," lived on it, were opposed by the "machine." But, as Doc Burton had warned, the machine is devised, produced, and run by people too. For the Steinbeck of *The Grapes of Wrath* (1939) the people responsible for the machine had surrendered to it their most vital and most valuable temperamental virtues. The most extreme generalization of this theme was that of the violent opposition of a cruel abstraction imposing itself upon a vivid and real concrete life. Animals prey upon each other; the strong eat the weak, or kill them for their pleasure. That this is a fascinating spectacle is testified in several of Steinbeck's stories, noticeably those of *The Long Valley* (1938). Both the intimate understanding of nature and the inhuman retreat from it are part of Steinbeck's point of view. The corresponding emotions are love of the land and indifference to it.

In his early novels, Steinbeck attempts to elaborate upon a rather simple thesis regarding these problems. *The Pastures of Heaven* (1932) wrestles with the problem of a mysterious fate which nullifies human aspiration and defiles human dignity. The restless succession of mishap and minor tragedy in that book testifies to a bewilderment over the meaning both of human hope and of the nemesis. *To a God Unknown* (1933) stresses to the point of boredom the theme of man's mystic relationship to the soil. In *Tortilla Flat* (1935), as later in *Cannery Row* (1945) and *The Wayward Bus* (1947), we are asked to view a type of life reduced to the level of animal cunning and a behavior charmingly and comically simple. It is only in *In Dubious Battle* and *The Grapes of Wrath* that Steinbeck tries for some clarification of his social view. The latter was his most ambitious, as it proved his most fabulously popular, book.

The design of that novel, long and verbose as it is, may be reduced to three observable strategies: the realistic, the symbolic, the philosophical. On the first level, Steinbeck was capable of effective writing. His representation in individual scenes (when viewed in isolation) is very impressive. For the most part, he resists the temptation to overreach his opportunities. The seriousness of human crisis and the comedy of everyday issues are often quite economically given. In such passages as the following, he reveals a lesson well learned from Hemingway:

Ahead of him, beside the road, a scrawny, dusty willow tree cast a speckled shade. Joad could see it ahead of him, its poor branches curving over the way, its load of leaves tattered and scraggly as a molting chicken. Joad was sweating now. His blue shirt darkened down his back and under his arms. He pulled at the visor of his cap and creased it in the middle, breaking its cardboard lining so completely that it could never look new again. And his steps took on new speed and intent toward the shade of the distant willow tree. At the willow he knew there would be shade, at least one hard bar of absolute shade thrown by the trunk, since the sun had passed its zenith.

At least here the details are self-contained; no one of them is incompatible with its very limited subject. And those sections of the *The Grapes of Wrath* which remain free of large and false implication contain within themselves a remarkably well sustained narrative—held together as it is by the simple but convincing structural device of U.S. Highway 66. The next strategy is less successful, though even here it is sometimes quite well integrated with the first. The symbolic exertions of the author are, for the most part, violations of theme rather than successful extensions of it. The turtle carries too much of a burden; the tractor violates more than the land; Rose of Sharon's gesture at the novel's end is a curiously inept survival of the sex-land mysticism of *To a God Unknown*. In general the symbols are embarrassingly and awkwardly intrusive; more than that, they are quite unnecessary Whitmanian raids upon the self-sufficient and concrete substance of the novel. Instead of emerging naturally and with due humility from the novel's material, they are added to it, or singled out from it for special, self-conscious attention.

The worst strategy of all, the philosophical, involves what are perhaps some of the most wretched violations of aesthetic taste observable in modern American fiction; they are the fictional version of Sandburg's strident *The People, Yes* (1936). For the most part they are contained within the fifteen short chapters of "philosophical" commentary, through which Steinbeck has tried to impose a false epic note upon what is basically a sound conception. Nor is he content merely to represent himself as a philosopher in these chapters; he occasionally also gives the Joads the privileges of the country sage. A study of the style, rhetoric, and intellectual content of the fifteen chapters reveals Steinbeck's writing at its worst and his mind at its most confused; trying, as he does so often, to stimulate the worst kind of intellectual pathos and to force the reader into a recognition of false significance:

. . . For man, unlike any other thing organic or inorganic in the universe, grows beyond his work, walks up the stairs of his concepts, emerges ahead of his accomplishments. This you may say of man—when theories change and crash, when schools, philosophies, when narrow dark alleys of thought, national, religious, economic, grow and disintegrate, man reaches, stumbles forward, painfully, mistakenly sometimes. Having stepped forward, he may slip back, but only half a step, never the full step back. This you may say and know it and know it.

Because this passage is so placed that we know Steinbeck intends it to be taken with the utmost seriousness, it is especially damaging in what it reveals of his intellectual poverty. That poverty of mind, which seems a common failure among a majority of naturalist writers, serves to weaken the effect of *The Grapes of Wrath* as a whole. This passage and its fellows, together with the inappropriate mutterings of Ma and Tom Joad and of Casy, force the reader away from what are the essentially good sections of the novel: those parts of it in which Steinbeck has exercised (almost unwittingly, it seems) the caution and factual decorum demanded by the material. Aside from the very quiet, subdued heroics of ordinary man in critical situations, there are the heroics forced upon him by an author unsure of his subject and confused over what he should make of it. They are indicative of a damning intellectual weakness in naturalist writing throughout the century—a weakness which has on many occasions reduced talent to the position of servant to a falsely rhetorical purpose. It has done worse damage to critics, who have more often than not insisted that a writer's work is only so significant as he himself intrusively says it is.

v

When, in 1929, William Faulkner came to the writing of that group of novels for which he is best known, he had already published three books as a farewell to his adolescence: two novels, *Soldiers' Pay* (1926), and *Mosquitoes* (1927), and a volume of poems, *The Marble Faun* (1924). In each of these he proved himself no more than a second-rate imitator of current or passing literary trends. There was nothing in this product of the 1920's that suggested he would be more than the postwar romantic and sophisticate that his plots and his neo-Paterian style indicated. *Soldiers' Pay* is full of echoes, from Pater, Wilde, and late Victorian poetry; *Mosquitoes* bears pathetic evidence of the pervasive influence in the American twenties of Aldous Huxley. Faulkner was, in short, the New Orleans bohemian that Sherwood Anderson had described him as being. He had his war record, as did his contemporaries; it was expected that the war experience would take its literary toll, as it actually had in *Soldiers' Pay*.

One important fact, however, did serve to divert his interest in the postwar mode: the South itself, and his own inheritance from its tradition. He turned neither to the habit of Southern pseudo-romanticism nor to the practice of using the Southern economy for leftist tractarian novels. Faulkner's life and his ancestral past led, rather, to another kind of fictional treatment. It was significant that he did not rush to New York to view the South from there or stay long in the Paris cafés where perspectives upon American culture were cheaply purchased, but chose rather to remain in the Mississippi region of his fathers.

That this region was important for his work even a cursory reading of it will reveal. But he was not satisfied with the superficial view of the South that clutters the novels, for example, of T. S. Stribling. Nor did it lend itself merely to the cloying rhetoric of such a treatment as Eudora Welty gives it. Faulkner may be said to have had a deep, an almost obsessive preoccupation with his region of the South. So that he might treat it with the imaginative freedom that it so richly deserved, he created his own county for his fiction. This Yoknapatawpha County of Mississippi provides a constant reminder of the real Southern world, and Faulkner defined it, bounded and surveyed it, with a statistical thoroughness which argued above all the literal accuracy necessary for the substantiation of his creative acts. As novel followed novel in the richly creative 1930's, the county acquired both breadth of reality and depth of treatment.

In the same decade the fiction written in the South reached its highest level of distinction; it divides itself with some accuracy into those novels written from a documentary bias and into those written from a preoccupation with the region, with regional peculiarities contributing to large (sometimes universal) moral concerns.[3] Erskine Caldwell and Faulkner best represent these two classes of Southern fiction. In the first group, the most conspicuous member, however, is T. S. Stribling, whose novels largely concern Southern political and economic conditions; most notable

[3] Other recent novelists include Carson McCullers, *The Heart is a Lonely Hunter* (1940), *The Member of the Wedding* (1946), and Truman Capote *Other Voices, Other Rooms* (1948). A full consideration of Southern fiction would also treat such novelists as Stark Young and Julia Peterkin. One of the best artists of fiction that the South has produced, Katherine Anne Porter, has confined her work to the short story and the novelette and should properly be treated in a study of shorter fiction.

For a discerning study of the division in Southern fiction I have indicated above, see Robert Penn Warren's essay, "T. S. Stribling: A Paragraph in the History of Critical Realism," in the *American Review*, February 1934, pages 463–86. See Chapter VII for a brief consideration of Warren's own novels.

among them is the trilogy which describes the Vaiden family from the Civil War to modern times: *The Forge* (1931), *The Store* (1932), a Pulitzer prize winner in 1933, and *Unfinished Cathedral* (1934). Among those novelists belonging to the group headed by Faulkner is Eudora Welty; although her best work has been done in the short story, she has published two novels, *The Robber Bridegroom* (1942) and *Delta Wedding* (1946).

Any survey of Faulkner's fiction demands consideration both of the full nature of his fictional county and of the formal approaches which he used to its meaning. The organization used by Russell Roth in *Perspective* (Summer 1949) offers a number of suggestions. Its principal strategy is to consider Faulkner's view of his world in terms of the heroes of his novels. The first of these is the aesthete, who assumes in part the qualities of Faulkner's immediate postwar concerns. He is the self-defeating two-dimensional Hamlet of the *Soldiers' Pay* South. He seems to rely chiefly upon a faded Romanticism (not Southern so much as *fin de siècle* English), and upon an evasive cleverness. He is terribly weak, as a creature of the literary imagination as well as in his role of observer of his region. It is only in the figure of the young Bayard Sartoris, in *Sartoris* (1929), that he begins to suggest an association with Faulkner's principal thematic concerns. Young Sartoris, returned from the first World War, can understand the South of his origins only in terms of the violence he has experienced in the air corps during the war. The machine serves him as an instrument to hasten the time of his violent death; he pushes aggressively forward in his drive toward that end. In this novel the obsessive complications of the post Civil War South are combined with the mechanically aggravated means toward violence of modern warfare. So young Sartoris goes to a violent death as an aviator, leaving a wife and a child to continue the Sartoris family into at least one more generation.

Yet Sartoris is, after all, so charged with the impact of the World War upon his creator that he scarcely satisfies as a Faulkner hero. It is in the character of Quentin Compson that the weaknesses of the aesthete are made brilliantly to bear upon Faulkner's view of the South. We see, in *The Sound and the Fury* (1929), that he has been sent to Harvard at the sacrifice of a large section of Compson land. More important, he sees himself and his family in terms of what in his distorted mind are the faded ends of a Southern tradition. That preoccupation is developed through his intricate and complex concern over the fallen state of his sister's virtue. Candace has not only lost her virginity; she has actually consented to marriage with a Northerner and a banker. Quentin strives heroically to prevent both of these tragedies; then, failing, he works through to his own romantic and psychologically strained interpretation of them. The novel reveals brilliantly the impotence of the aesthete in his efforts both to understand his South and to act in terms of his understanding of it. In this connection, Quentin Compson's role in *Absalom, Absalom!* (1936) has its significant bearing upon the world of Faulkner's fiction. The story of the South which that novel so intricately tells is that of the rhetorical and psychological source of Quentin's obsessive search for the definition of his own relationship to it. In a room in Cambridge, in the "iron-grey New England winter," Quentin debates, constructs, and tries to formulate the meaning of the narrative of Colonel Sutpen's conquest of the South. He is assisted in this effort by Shreve McCannon, his Canadian roommate, who prods him, irritates him, exasperates him into statement, takes over the narrative from him and goads him into a climactic protestation concerning his attitude toward the South. This is the most complete development of the young aesthete's point of view; he is as violently thorough in his preoccupation with his tradition as he is impotent to grasp its meaning.

The second point of view is what we may call the "good weak hero." It is necessary to understand what both "good" and "weak" mean in this context. The goodness is partly a virtue of the will and intention; put simply, it is a desire to help. It involves its own kind of penetration beneath the traditional surface of things, its own frightening recognition of the evil which exists there. The weakness is a weakness of moral constitution. The hero of this second phase does not misunderstand, as do Bayard Sartoris and Quentin Compson; he understands all too well, beyond the power of effective action. There are three principal representatives of this type of hero: Horace Benbow of *Sartoris* and of *Sanctuary* (1931), Byron Bunch of *Light in August* (1932) and V. K. Ratliff of *The Hamlet* (1940). They are quite different in their reactions. Benbow is a transitional figure; we find him, in *Sartoris,* more the aesthete than anything else. He has failed in his marriage and in his conventional civic responsibilities. But he has an inviolable moral integrity which will not let him either gloss over a condition or escape it by ignoring it. His integrity, it can be seen, is partly the reason why he will not be able to rescue Lee Goodwin from an unjust death, nor defeat that archdemon of modern evil, Popeye. Byron Bunch is similarly ineffectual, though here it is his simplicity of mind and spirit which defeats him. He is simply not capable of penetrating or grasping the complex and obsessive world of violence which surrounds Joe Christmas and Joanna Burden. He can only intuitively comprehend and helplessly admire the undefiled and impervious goodness of Lena Grove.

Entirely different from both of these, Ratliff is Faulkner's "rational man," as John Arthos has called him, and in his person Faulkner has explored the possibilities and the limitations of a rational mind in its relation to the world of Yoknapatawpha County. Ratliff is a rational observer of the cunning and amoral skill of the Snopes invasion of that county. He is shrewd, as are the Snopeses; he understands the skills required to put over a "good deal"; he is, moreover, a folk comic spirit, able to interpret the progress of the Snopeses with the shrewd, folk insight of Frenchman's Bend. But his rational view is too pure to be effective. He can appeal to the victims of Snopes treachery only on that irritatingly sober plane of recognizably intelligent behavior. This point of view is ineffectual because, as Faulkner points out, victim conspires with villain in the Snopes triumph over the county. In the driving anxiety of Henry Armstid to buy his horse at whatever cost to him and his wife, the irrational urge toward such victimization is most thoroughly described. Ratliff ends his attempts to save the victims from themselves on a note of exasperation:

". . . I wasn't protecting a Snopes from Snopeses; I wasn't even protecting a people from a Snopes. I was protecting something that wasn't even a people, that wasn't nothing but something that dont want nothing but to walk and feel the sun and wouldn't know how to hurt no man even if it would and wouldn't want to even if it could, just like I wouldn't stand by and see you steal a meat-bone from a dog. I never made them Snopeses and I never made the folks that cant wait to bare their backsides to them. I could do more, but I wont. I wont, I tell you!"

In *Go Down, Moses* (1942) we are prepared for still a third, and the most recent Faulkner hero—the "good, strong man." This man is neither inept nor self-delusive in his approach to the problems of Yoknapatawpha County. He understands, he judges, he acts. He has first to go through an initiating ritual of understanding. The land must mean something beyond the values put upon it by bankers and realtors. He must see clearly through the craft and cunning of the Snopes tribe, but he must also be able to grapple with the problem which Ratliff was incapable of solving. The South has its own burdens, as it has its own culture. The burdens must be borne in its own way and without the ignorant and intrusive help of New England or Washington, D. C. It must be saved from itself as much as from its enemies who would wish to legislate its tradition out of existence. For the task of understanding all of this and acting upon it, Faulkner created Gavin Stevens, of *Intruder in the Dust* (1948) and *Knight's Gambit* (1949). He is learned, strong-natured and offensively garrulous. He asserts his distinction through the Phi Beta Kappa key which accompanies him on trips into the county and through an immense store of allusion and rhetoric. He is a kind of amateur detective, given to melodramatic surprises in the courtroom; he has a keen nose for corpses and can make the most skillful inferences from the appearance of churchyards and lonely shacks. In short, Faulkner has changed over from the strategy of aesthetic inference to the bald techniques of overt rhetorical statement. The initiation rites of the young boy of "The Bear" in *Go Down, Moses* had implicit in them all of the cultural requirements of a generative ideology. Responsibilities such as Faulkner imagines do not move from one generation to another by word of mouth alone. So too, in *Intruder in the Dust,* the cultural view of young Charles

Mallison must mature through experience. With his Negro friend and little old Miss Habersham, he must courageously accept the challenge in the scornful eyes of Lucas Beauchamp. But, though he does so, the actual journey to conviction is finally achieved through his having almost literally taken over Stevens' point of view, with all its rhetorical embellishments.

What distinguishes Faulkner from most of his fellow Southerners is his preoccupation with form. Though there is every possible difference between his work and that of Henry James, no novelist since James has developed so skillfully a genuinely effective management of point of view. Each of his novels since 1929 may be said to have made its own peculiar contribution to the history of literary form. Faulkner does not, therefore, merely "tell a story"; nor is he concerned, as many critics have insisted, merely with exploiting the horror, vulgarity and obscenity associated with the South's decadence. He is, above all, preoccupied with the problem of defining psychologically the moral sensibilities of his world.

The most brilliant example of Faulkner's experiments with point of view is, of course, *The Sound and the Fury*. In many ways, this novel is a more honest and efficient use of the so-called "stream of consciousness" technique than Joyce's notorious *Ulysses*. Unlike Joyce, Faulkner does not waste the method simply for the sake of virtuosity. The points of view of Benjy and Quentin Compson which direct the narrative in the novel's first two sections are consistently relevant; the discoveries and the interpretations of events of which each is capable are integrally pertinent to the narrative. Their value is seen only ultimately, when, in the full maturity of Faulkner's omniscience, the narrative concludes objectively. To have told the story in strictly chronological terms would have canceled out the advantages of Benjy's and Quentin's own special and varied insights into its meaning.

The other great marks of Faulkner's talent have to do with his conception of time and his very complex moral insight into his characters. The past is for Faulkner cumulatively and complexly relevant to the present. Each of his novels, whatever method it uses, testifies to the skill with which he has portrayed time as a psychological and moral complex in the vision of his characters. The intricate uses of time in *Absalom, Absalom!* eventually prove the meaning of that novel to be resident in the tortured consciousness of Quentin Compson. Every turn and return which the narrative takes provides a contribution to the uses he ultimately makes of the Sutpen story. The plotting of *Light in August* is more complex and less thoroughly integrated; there are so many diverse approaches to the problems centered in the violence of Joe Christmas's death that some remain unused and unresolved. But only Gavin Stevens is an exception to the general structural practice in the novel. As in his future roles, Stevens interferes with the novel's context, and violates its texture, for the sake of overt and intrusive speculation. *Sanctuary,* alleged to be a potboiler novel, has the least intricate of Faulkner's formal strategies; it is almost a straightforward narrative. But even here Faulkner is working in diverse points of view and in a variety of literary approaches.

Throughout, Faulkner exercises a substantial control over his work. No novel is without its evidences of auctorial discipline. This control is seen principally in its domination over the language in which the narrative is given. Much has been said about the extremes of obscurity and the unnecessary complication of that language, and there is undoubtedly some truth in the suggestion that Faulkner suffered from his isolation from fellow-workers in the craft. The excesses of Faulkner's style are perhaps most unfortunately seen in the way in which the texture of his prose of *Intruder in the Dust* violates the context of that novel. But there is no question of the general effectiveness of his style; it is not designed to make simple facts obscure but to give honestly the sub-surface complexities of his subjects. And there is considerably more versatility in the style of his work than is usually admitted. The pattern of the language in this passage, which opens the last section of *The Sound and the Fury*, is a brilliant example of Faulkner's skill:

The day dawned bleak and chill. A moving wall of grey light out of the northeast which, instead of dissolving into moisture, seemed to disintegrate into minute and venomous particles, like dust that, when Dilsey opened the door of the cabin and emerged, needled laterally into her flesh, precipitating not so much a moisture as a substance partaking of the quality of thin, not quite congealed oil. She wore a stiff black straw hat perched upon her turban, and a maroon velvet cape with a border of mangy and anonymous fur above a dress of purple silk, and she stood in the door for awhile with her myriad and sunken face lifted to the weather, and one gaunt hand flac-soled as the belly of a fish, then she moved the cape aside and examined the bosom of her gown.

In another sense, the passage which follows, from *The Wild Palms* (1939), demonstrates a disciplined control over the essential meaning of the tall convict's relationship to the rampaging river. It bears an attitude toward the material which is not satisfied with the surface articulation of which the convict is capable, but must probe further, to make articulate what he cannot himself put into words.

It was mud he lay upon, but it was solid underneath, it was earth, it did not move; if you fell upon it you broke your bones against its incontrovertible passivity sometimes, but it did not accept you substanceless and enveloping and suffocating, down and down and down; it was hard at times to drive a plough through, it sent you spent, weary, and cursing its light-long insatiable demands, back to your bunk at sunset at times, but it did not snatch you violently out of all familiar knowing and sweep you, thrall and impotent, for days against any returning.

Finally, the passage below suggests quite convincingly Faulkner's use of the comical that exists in his material. The comedy of his characters and his region, like the morbid extensions of its horror, is never exploited for its own sake, but rather, related closely with a total complex of meanings.

They saw the horse the Texan had given them whirl and dash back and rush through the gate into Mrs. Littlejohn's yard and run up the front steps and crash once on the wooden veranda and vanish through the front door. Eck and the boy ran up onto the veranda. A lamp sat on a table just inside the door. In its mellow light they saw the horse fill the long hallway like a pinwheel, gaudy, furious and thunderous. A little further down the hall there was a varnished yellow melodeon. The horse crashed into it; it produced a single note, almost a chord, in bass, resonant and grave, of deep and sober astonishment; the horse with its monstrous and antic shadow whirled again and vanished through another door.

vi

The fiction of Thomas Wolfe has its own persuasive rhetoric. It is more ambitious, more voluminous, and more nakedly and powerfully eccentric than any other in the his-

tory of the American novel. Wolfe believed firmly in the
art of "inclusion"; and, although he worried throughout
his career about the problem of establishing an objective
surveillance over his creations, he cannot, even with the
help of his good-willed editors, be said to have solved that
problem. One of the most significant documents for the
theoretical view of modern fiction is a letter Wolfe wrote
(1937) to F. Scott Fitzgerald, in answer to Fitzgerald's rather
too primly severe objections to Wolfe's writing:

You say that the great writer like Flaubert has consciously left
out the stuff that Bill or Joe will come along presently and put
in. Well, don't forget, Scott, that a great writer is not only a
leaver-outer but also a putter-inner, and that Shakespeare and
Cervantes and Dostoevsky were great putter-inners—greater putter-inners, in fact, than taker-outers and will be remembered for
what they put in—remembered, I venture to say, as long as Mon-
sieur Flaubert will be remembered for what he left out.
. . . .
As to the rest of it in your letter about cultivating an alter ego,
becoming a more conscious artist, my pleasantness or grief, exuberance or cynicism, and how nothing stands out in relief because everything is keyed at the same emotional pitch. . . . Let
the Fadimans and De Votos do that kind of talking but not
Scott Fitzgerald. . . . I want to be a better artist. I want to be a
more selective artist. . . . I want to use such talent as I have, control such forces as I may own, direct such energy as I may use
more clearly, more surely and to better purpose. But Flaubert
me no Flauberts, Bovary me no Bovarys, Zola me no Zolas. And
exuberance me no exuberances. Leave this stuff for those who
huckster in it and give me, I pray you, the benefits of your fine
intelligence and your high creative faculties, all of which I so
genuinely and profoundly admire. . . .

There is no doubt that Wolfe was the great "putter-
inner" of contemporary American fiction. No writer had
greater difficulty with the formal problems of the art of fic-

tion, and no writer was so compulsively driven to "put in". There is the well-known story of the author in his New York flat writing endlessly and voluminously, covering numerous sheets of paper, and filling two packing cases with reams of pencilled manuscript. The role of his editors has also been told and retold—of their work with scissors and paste, their advice and their encouragement. This product, put together in four principal books, constituted an overflowing of Wolfe's experience into a reckless and superabundant review of one American's search for spiritual definition. The whole of it was autobiographical to an excessive degree and in an obsessively peculiar way. Discussing this problem of the range of the auctorial ego in fiction, Wolfe had this to say in his *The Story of a Novel* (1936):

As I have said, my conviction is that all serious creative work must be at bottom autobiographical, and that a man must use the material and experience of his own life if he is to create anything that has substantial value. . . .

. . . .

In spite of this, it is impossible for a man who has the stuff of creation in him to make a literal transcription of his own experience. Everything in a work of art is changed and transfigured by the personality of the artist. And as far as my own first book is concerned, I can truthfully say that I do not believe that there is a single page of it that is true to fact.

What Wolfe meant by "the personality of the artist" (it is significant that the word "artist" occupies a subordinate place in the phrase) was perhaps the "presiding genius" which watched over the birth, life, and death of his creatures. Probably also, reincarnation—for they recur and are renamed before they resume their journeys. The first ego-centrality of his long narrative is called Eugene Gant. *Look*

Homeward, Angel (1929) is the story of his parents, his boy-hood, and of the initial phase of his revolt against the world of Altamont, Catawba. The father and mother make supple-mentary contributions to his development; and the turmoil of the Gant family dissensions serves roughly to form his early view. He moves from them to the state university, after having enjoyed an enthusiastic if scarcely disciplined intro-duction to literature and language at "The Altamont Fit-ting School," the Leonards' private school. At the end of the novel, Eugene has broken with his family in a violent scene of bitter recrimination, and sets out on his pilgrimage.

The search is, above all, for a literary resolution of the tortures of adolescent experience. The obvious place to go is Harvard; *Of Time and the River* (1935) takes him there. He devours the library and absorbs learning as he had ear-lier assimilated physical experience. In the classes of Pro-fessor Hatcher (Baker's "47 Workshop"), he struggles with the disciplines of playwriting; outside the halls of learning, he makes several friends and exploits his relationship with the fabulous and absurd Uncle Bascom Pentland. He re-turns to Altamont for the funeral of his father, then starts his brief career as instructor of English in a night school branch of a New York university. At the conclusion of this novel, he makes a tour of Europe, where he learns more about himself than about the world he visits. As the novel closes, he is once more on his way to America, his funds exhausted.

At this point in the narrative, Wolfe decided that he needed to shift his ground. In the hope that he might achieve greater objectivity in his narrative, he abandoned Eugene Gant, returned to the North Carolina of his youth, and once more took up the narrative of his life. The entire manuscript of *Look Homeward, Angel* had in the beginning been written in the first person; the "I" changed to "Eugene," then to "George." But the pattern, once resumed, was not substantially altered; and after a recapitulation of the North Carolina themes, Gant-Webber resumes his career in New York from the point of the end of the second novel. *The Web and the Rock* (1939) thus retraces in part the matter of *Look Homeward, Angel,* and continues the narrative of *Of Time and the River.* The fourth and concluding book, *You Can't Go Home Again* (1940), brings the career of Gant-Webber almost up to date; Webber's success as a novelist, his relationship with Foxhall Edwards, his editor, and the break from him, the return to his home town, now in the throes of calamitous depression, and the final trip to Germany—these are all a recapitulation of Wolfe's own life and career. Though the last two volumes were published posthumously and by a different publisher, it is obvious that the major effort at objectivity in their account is Wolfe's own. Webber is an uglier Gant, and a less egotistically regarded character. The natural excesses of Eugene's figure are exaggerated still further in Webber's. The hatefulness of Eugene's self-absorption is accentuated in the riotously ugly love affair that Webber has with Esther Jack in *The Web and the Rock.* These are the measure of Wolfe's efforts to provide more objective treatment. The objectivity is discernible only at isolated points, in shifts of Wolfe's attitude toward his characters, and in the more subdued treatment of Webber's boyhood.

Aside from this question (and it is, after all, the major one, whatever protests Wolfe may have made to his critics and editors), there is the matter of what he actually wanted to do with these materials. He wished, energetically and vainly, to make from quantity a qualitative assertion concerning the meaning of life in its American cultural setting.

It was a difficult thing to do, and Wolfe was especially handicapped by the almost incredible energy of raw creation which resisted formulation and ordering. Far from addressing himself to the task of composition, he submitted the responsibilities of such a task to his editors, especially to Maxwell Perkins. "For the crucial act of the artist," says Mark Schorer, "the unique act which is composition, a sympathetic editorial blue pencil and scissors were substituted." It is not that Wolfe was unaware of the necessities involved in that act; we all know that he wrestled violently with them. Rather, he was temperamentally incapable of controlling his verbal energy and was as much liable to further expansion as he was to cutting in his maneuvers at revision. Over and above all of this, the act of composition should have occurred, at least in its initial, disciplinary stages, at the time of the writing itself; it should not have been forced upon him afterward but should have come from an inner compulsion toward form. Similarly, his imitative excursions into the possibilities of Joyce's form and themes were scarcely rewarding, but merely added on to his own abundant inventiveness a specious and strangely intrusive element.

Consequently, his work has an incredible mixture of the most impressive with the worst possible writing. All of his characters are giants of appetite and behavior; they exaggerate each of their traits through an excess of rhetoric and an obsessive duplication. His descriptions are richly diverse and crowded with sensuous detail; lust for food, drink, and experience is fused with a "yearning of the spirit."[4] The energy of Wolfe's expression contrasts sadly with the pov-

4 The "hunger" of Wolfe's youth seems often indiscriminately to be for physical experience and "spiritual" meaning; he suffers from a violent confusion of appetite, which often fails to discriminate between food and conviction.

erty of intellect with which he at crucial moments tries to give it a culminating significance. The passages which follow illustrate these two aspects of his work. The first is from *Look Homeward, Angel,* and reveals Wolfe's appetitive excitement over sensuous detail:

They fed stupendously. Eugene began to observe the food and the seasons. In the autumn, they barrelled huge frosty apples in the cellar. Gant bought whole hogs from the butcher, returning home early to salt them, wearing a long work-apron, and rolling his sleeves half up his lean hairy arms. Smoked bacons hung in the pantry, the great bins were full of flour, the dark recessed shelves groaned with preserved cherries, peaches, plums, quinces, apples, pears. All that he touched waxed in rich pungent life: his Spring gardens, wrought in the black wet earth below the fruit trees, flourished in huge crinkled lettuces that wrenched cleanly from the loamy soil with small black clots stuck to their crisp stocks; fat red radishes; heavy tomatoes.

The second, from *Look Homeward, Angel,* is an example of the rich but confused rhetoric of which Wolfe is so often guilty:

His life was like that river, rich with its own deposited and onward-borne agglutinations, fecund with its sedimental accretions, filled exhaustlessly by life in order to be more richly itself, and this life, with the great purpose of a river, he emptied now into the harbor of his house, the sufficient haven of himself, for whom the gnarled vines wove round him thrice, the earth burgeoned with abundant fruit and blossom, the fire burnt madly.

7

THE LAST TEN YEARS

i

THE American novel of the 1940's may be studied in at least four ways. There is, first, the novel of World War II, with its symptomatic indebtedness to almost all of the fictional tendencies of the previous three decades. Then there is the spectacle of the established novelist who continues to exploit those characteristics which originally helped to establish his reputation. There is also the persistence of naturalism in recent fiction—a naturalism indebted both to the pioneers of the century's beginnings and to the novels of the 1930's. Finally, some few recent novels have indicated an indebtedness to a growing critical concern with form in modern fiction.

Considering even a selection from the abundance of war fiction from 1943 on, one discovers a number of facts concerning it. Intellectually, these novelists seem less naïve about war than were their elders of another war generation.

They are victims of a kind of ideological battle fatigue; the cynicism of their characters is less the result of world-weariness than of ignorance. If the propaganda mills grind less thoroughly, the generation writing about the second World War are less naïvely abused by the collapse of values, as they are less impressed by values of any sort. There is in these novels an explicit and implicit criticism of American culture that reaches deep into the leftist attitudes of the thirties. We discover also supplementary impressions of the twentieth-century Grand Tour of the common soldier. From North Africa to Italy to France, leading usually to Paris, the central attraction for the American, this invasion of Europe's cities has the quality of an inverted pilgrimage. The American soldier visits Rome, Florence, and other classical centers of Italian life, feeling dirty, abused, and bored. He is the fashioner of a violent dislocation of Italian life, but pinpoint bombing and long-range destruction scarcely give him a clear notion of what it is he is invading.

The novelists of World War II have been concerned in part with the portrayal of this boredom and with the isolation of intelligence which comes from a large-scale military pilgrimage to strange lands. The year 1943 is scarcely the year 1914; the novelists of the second war have hardly a sense of the collapse of a tradition. The great majority of the characters who inhabit these novels consider the second World War an interruption of their privacy, and a dangerous interference with their normal lives. Hemingway's Krebs ("Soldier's Home") had found life in his Kansas town strange and unbearable after World War I; the characters of the later fiction bring with them their image of Kansas, purified of its more unpleasant facts, and hold to it throughout long stretches of boredom punctuated intermittently by violence.

The persistent impression given by these novelists is of a dirty and inconvenient break in the rhythm of the prewar life. Only occasionally does the rhetoric of purpose intervene. There are some latter-day conceptions of "mission," but even these are assumed without either the crusading fervor of Mrs. Wharton's or the negativist attitude of Hemingway's heroes. If desertion is not a major theme in this fiction (as it was in the earlier war novel), neither are ideological heroics. All of which is to say that the novels of the second World War are more honestly literal in their perspective upon events. There are exceptions of course; but these are written chiefly by men whose view of the war has been influenced by perspectives gained in another time: Irwin Shaw's *The Young Lions* (1948) in a deeply sincere, almost literal acceptance of the ideological moralities of the 1930's; Glenway Wescott's *Apartment in Athens* (1945) in a special view of civilization; and John Steinbeck's *The Moon Is Down* (1942) in a tender concern over persons of whatever national or ideological complexion.

Shaw's *The Young Lions* (1948) is the most ambitious of these three. It is long, earnest, and loosely constructed. Its principal narrative responsibilities are carried by the Jewish soldier, Noah Ackerman, the man from Broadway and Hollywood, Michael Whitacre, and a German sergeant, Christian Diestl. Through these and scores of other characters the war is brought to the men who fought it, who combine in their persons both the immediate details and the importunate ideological issues of the conflict. Noah has first to fight his way to recognition as a person at his Florida army base; he then becomes the principal bearer of Shaw's earnest purpose, proves to be hard, courageous, and tender. In the end he is killed by Diestl, who is in turn wiped out by Whitacre. There is nothing in the novel which is not

treated with the utmost seriousness by its author; but, although there are a few finely realized incidents, the association of particular with brooding generalization is most
often accomplished in some such fashion as this, as Michael
Whitacre observes the effect of Pearl Harbor on California
citizens:

Are these the people, created in greatness by the work of Jeffer-
son and Franklin, he thought, are these the bitter farmers and
hunters and craftsmen who came out of the wilderness, furious
for liberty and justice, is this the new world of giants sung by
Whitman?

The only link between these observations, which are
Shaw's, not Whitacre's, and the character is in the words
"he thought."

Both Whitacre and Ackerman follow through the events
of the European phase of World War II, from beginning to
end, dominated by the tender concerns and disarming skepticism that Shaw had earlier shown in his plays; but the
overwhelming disorder, chaos, and filth of the war itself
almost completely destroys the hope of seeing "an America
of friends and neighbors, an America in which a man could
finally put away his over-civilized doubts, his book-soured
cynicism, his realistic despair, and humbly and gratefully
lose himself." Shaw apparently wanted to produce a work
as large and as broad as the war itself. *The Young Lions* is
appropriately supplied with an abundance of events, both
large and small in importance. Some of them, and the persons who figure in them, have no discernible relevance to
the narrative and either are dropped or vanish in the on-
rushing sequence of incidents. Many of them are violently
yoked by coincidence; still others are forced to serve the
author's rhetorical purpose. Had Shaw made a novel from

the suggestion offered by the Dover minister to his congregation one Sunday, the result might have been much more successful as a revelation of the war's meaning:

"How does a soldier love his enemy? I say it is this way—to kill sparingly and with a sense of sin and tragedy, sin that is yours equally with the sin of the man who falls at your hands."

Something of that ambiguity of evil does come through the accumulation of detail: the Jew-baiting in the Florida camp, the complexity of Lieutenant Hardenburg's feelings and acts, the neurotic evil of behind-the-scenes Berlin, the remarks of Bruce, the Negro servant in Whiteacre's California home. But over all this there is the driving necessity for significance and purposeful commentary, all of it quite close to the surface of the narrative. And the book's worst fault is its failure to contain and to use detail in any disciplined way. Variations of style and structure are additional evidence of the book's weakness of conception. There is much too much of everything except a sense of form and a clarity of definition.

The form and style of these war novels reflect the eager apprenticeship served in the modern American school. The simplicity of diction, of dialogue, and of character reading established by Hemingway becomes an accepted manner. No more excellent example of that pervasive influence is seen than in the starkly simple representation of the war in Harry Brown's *A Walk in the Sun* (1944). Here the meaning and the necessity of the war in an isolated segment of a secondary attack are skillfully confined. The elements of chance and risk, the problems of minute-by-minute adjustment to emergency, the dynamics of fear and courage, are all unpretentiously given. The novel lacks the kind of interpretation which Lieutenant Henry had given the Caporetto retreat in *A Farewell to Arms*. There are no outbursts of violated dignity in Brown's representation, only a rather quiet explanation of immediate emotions and strategies.

There are more ambitious and more pretentious novels, of course; and the authors of these try to take advantage of the large fictional strategies made popular by Dos Passos in *U.S.A.* John Horne Burns's *The Gallery* (1947) may lay claim to his own inventive variant upon those strategies. The focal center of the novel's form is the Galleria Umberto of Naples. From it the action moves back to the North African and forward to the Italian theater; to it the narrative invariably returns. The strategy is skillfully chosen but eventually leads more to a confusion than to a definition of events. Its purpose seems to be to portray the inevitable dislocations which occur in a large-scale military offensive. The Americans are almost always presented in unflattering terms; they are usually either naïve or cynical. In any event they carry with them the imperfections of character and mind derived from the American setting, and these seem strangely dislocated in Naples.

The most ambitious, as the most popular, of World War II novels is Norman Mailer's *The Naked and the Dead* (1948). This novel is carefully planned and shrewdly formed. The setting provides its own limitations upon the action and its treatment; it is a small South Pacific island, which the Americans must take on their slow progress toward Japan. For the duration of the novel, the war is narrowed to this pinpoint of its global strategy. But, unlike the persistent tedium of Thomas Heggen's good ship *Reluctant*, in the novel *Mister Roberts* (1946), this island contains every opportunity for action, and every risk of death. Having rather painstakingly explained the military prob-

lem involved, Mailer addresses himself to the task of revealing the personalities engaged in this action. Anopopei
is linked with Texas and San Francisco and every other
American locality from which the men have come. Their
American backgrounds have an intimate bearing upon their
behavior, and these backgrounds are given in detail. The
bulk of the novel is traceable to this earnest desire to provide the minutiae of motive and cultural past from which
the present action takes its incentive. The intellectual content of the novel is considerable; in the postponements
which characterize an action of this kind, Mailer has the
opportunity to explore motives large and small. A major
conflict of motives exists between Lieutenant Herne and
General Cummings. Herne's liberalism and skepticism are
a convincing record of the latter-day career of leftist training in the 1930's; on the other hand, the ideological motives
of the General seem to have derived from a long-term in-
doctrination by the military mind. Both characters suffer a
kind of frustration, the General's accidental—he is not present when the victory is achieved—the Lieutenant's imposed
upon him in a scouting mission in which he meets his death.
What makes this aspect of the novel convincing is the author's caution in proportioning space to the intellectual
aspects of the event. No generalization is without at least
some attempt at concrete and precise expression. The actions are undertaken from a motive substantially reduced
to individual contexts of feeling; they achieve a particu-
larity that is usually appropriate to their circumstances.
Throughout they are supplemented by the details of their
setting and of the range of personalities involved. Under
these circumstances of fictional representation, there is little
risk that the novel will suffer from any kind of oversimplification. We cannot say that it is a criticism of the military

mind or that it is a reflection upon the weaknesses of the liberal position opposed to it, because it is both of these things, and it is many other things besides. There is no room, therefore, for the specious bitterness of Robert Lowry's *Casualty* (1946), or the sentimental attachment to vaguely sensed human values which give such a strangely anticlimactic quality to Burns's *The Gallery* and Alfred Hayes' *The Girl on the Via Flaminia* (1949). If *The Naked and the Dead* can be criticized, it is for an oversupply of serious intention. Despite the very shrewd original strategy of form, its intention is overweighted by detail; the novel has an embarrassing wealth of supporting particulars. Its very discretion of plan becomes excessive because too heavily insisted upon.

One needs also, of course, to consider the war from the point of view of those civilians who suffered it either within or away from the combat area. American novelists did not neglect this subject. The civilian life during or directly after the war is the theme of several novels, most of them of indifferent worth, and many of them concerned with the Washington merry-go-round and its effect on the personal lives of secretaries and sub-administrators. Rarely did a novel see and present the war as a critical end-result of the doctrinal tensions of the 1930's; such a novel is Irwin Stark's *The Invisible Island* (1948), whose merit lies in the integrity and precision of much of its style. The hero, Matthew Stratton, is a 4-F; he has been made so because of a beating taken during a political riot. His injury is in this sense an ideological consequence of the late 1930's. Mr. Stark's novel is a product of all of the doctrinal issues and pressures of that decade, as well as an earnest imitation of manners made popular then by Farrell, Dos Passos, Wolfe, and others. The structure of the novel consists of two sequences: that of the

present, in which Stratton works in a Negro school, a rather
large fee paid to his social conscience; and that of the bio-
graphical past, through which the Stratton of the present is
explained. The past and present alternate with what has
obviously been intended as a very shrewd and strategic relevance. The pertinent influence of past on present is designed
to explain a man's partial commitment to social action,
which throughout the novel is defined as a moral necessity.
Stratton is portrayed with a more than ordinarily sensitive
attention to what in the thirties and forties may be called
the "hesitant social man." Throughout he is convinced that
he ought to be a writer, that his art has an exclusive importance; but that conviction is frequently undermined by
events and by the relation to them of his most cherished
friends. The Spanish Civil War is such an event, and there
are many others. His decision, therefore, to teach in a Negro
school has an extraordinary relevance. In those sequences
in which Stark describes his hero "trying to understand" his
pupils there is very fine prose. He has not only to contend
with an almost hopeless slum morale; he must as a white
man gain the confidence of boys who are, and feel deeply
that they are, his racial and cultural enemies. Stratton's perception of the hopeless complexity of this task and his devotion to it are an exceptional and gratifyingly perceptive
treatment of a subject generally botched by superficial handling. The novel has many faults; Stark writes overzealously,
often presents intellectual matter too superficially, quite
frequently offers only a patchwork integration of events.
But it is one of a very few novels in the last decade which
have remained relatively free of the devastating clichés of
social and political realism.

Fictional studies of "the liberation" in Europe and of
civilian disasters have grown in number. Notorious (for its

sales) among them is John Hersey's *The Wall* (1950), a fictional account of the extermination of Warsaw Jews from
1939 to 1943. The value of Mr. Hersey's novel is that of
minute and relentless documentation; there is no extenuation of data, and Mr. Hersey should perhaps be applauded
for this fact. Nor is there any alleviation from tedious
duplication of minutiae. A morally significant truth, un-
sentimentally documented, is in itself valuable for its admonitory influence upon the reader; one does not, however, make the truth more significant by ceaseless reiteration. More skillful is Albert Guerard's *Night Journey*
(1950), which discusses the occupation with all of the technical advantage a student of Joseph Conrad must have over
his naturalist contemporaries. The prose has an agreeable
modesty and economy. The shifting of point of view relates
largely and pertinently to the moral question of the hero's
troubled insights into the behavior of his superior officer.
The moral issue has to do with the treatment of a town
in liberated country. In this interesting adaptation of Conrad's point-of-view studies of moral ambiguity, Guerard has
certainly found a more profound and a less sentimental
method than those which made the novels of Hersey (*A
Bell for Adano*, 1944) and Hayes best-sellers. The most
remarkable novel of this type so far published is that by
John Hawkes (*The Cannibal*); it is a surrealist evocation of
European despair. Its setting is that of a symbolically grue-
some postwar dislocation. All of the pathological consequences of war are here given within an extraordinarily
circumscribed fictional area. The single American officer is
killed by patriots of a liberated German town. The murder
sets this Germany free—though it is perhaps incorrect to call
it either Germany or free. The culminating morbidity of the
tale is that event from which it takes its title: the Duke, after

much trouble, finally captures a young boy, whom he kills and prepares to eat—the myth of Tereus and Philomela deprived of all passion and relevance. The novel is so irrevocably dominated by this and by other enormities that it remains a remote and terrible fantasy, without any of the profound significance of Kafka's fiction, into whose company Mr. Guerard (in his enthusiastic introduction) insists it be admitted.

The Cannibal (1949) is a testimony to a small but persistent struggle on the part of recent novelists to break away from the naturalist impasse. It is in a sense a part of the struggle against naturalism; naturalistic only in its surface details, it depends upon such poignant accuracy of particulars for the ground of its persuasion. Its secret lies elsewhere. There were years of modern American fiction during which the novel had to be one of two things: either raw documentation or indifferent fantasy. The facts of World War I had either to be frankly faced (mud, stench, and blood profanely tolerated and stoically endured) or entirely ignored. It was Hemingway or Cabell—or nothing. World War II also has its documentation, with superfluous commentary upon a fixed and prior assumption. Hersey's *The Wall* and Shaw's *The Young Lions* are cases in point. The novel of John Hawkes cuts through both document and discourse, to reach another and symbolic level of meaning.

ii

The established novelists of both the 1920's and the 1930's had great difficulty extending and consolidating their reputations during the decade of the second World War. There is an overwhelming impression in most cases of a form and approach once successful, now being exploited again and again with diminishing effectiveness. The work of John Dos Passos on his second trilogy was finished with the publication of *The Grand Design*. In the trilogy of which this is the last novel, he abandoned the more obvious of his technical curiosities and he tried also to write political narrative. The novels are a measure of Dos Passos' dissatisfaction with the three principal political formulations of the thirties: the communist point of view and strategy are rejected in *Adventures of a Young Man* (1939); the character of native fascism is explored in *Number One* (1943); New Deal Washington is portrayed in *The Grand Design* (1948). These separate portrayals are unified through the attention paid to the Spotswood family, but Dos Passos quite clearly shows that no member of that family ideally serves as a locus of his social criticism. The death of Glenn Spotswood appeared, in the first novel, to have underscored his author's "tragic view" of leftist morality; but in the last novel, that death is exploited and misunderstood by Spotswood's father, now become a popular liberal radio commentator, who is in turn used by the party responsible for Glenn's death. As for Tyler Spotswood, publicity agent and political advisor of Mr. "Number One," he too is affected by Glenn's heroics, but in *The Grand Design* he sadly appears as a drunken and defeated "lost soul."

The character of Dos Passos' ideological misery in this trilogy is different from that of the grim documentation of *U.S.A.* His novels become an earnest attempt to dramatize the ironic disparity between political good will and corrupt reality. Perhaps their most impressive result is their portrayal of the confusion which visits men of good will in the open arena of party strategies and political event. But there is more than that, in the last two novels at least. The refrain which accompanies all of the narratives in these novels is his own version of the democratic lyric. The nature of this refrain was first revealed in the Preface to the one-volume edition of *U.S.A.* (1938). Dos Passos' world view is still panoramic; the country is made up of many people, who have many views and hopes, and suffer many defeats. The novels themselves point up the failures of the thirties to give political definition or organization to their varied and fluctuant wishes. There is a liberal character who suffers less from Dos Passos' tender-hearted cynicism than any other. He is the honest, deeply sincere man, who brings his special knowledge and his inexpertly orientated "liberal" devotion to Mr. Roosevelt's Washington. But he is a pathetic creature at best, not because he is not efficient in his specialized work but because he is politically naïve and quite incapable of altering the evil course of political organization. Throughout, the fiction published by Dos Passos in the 1940's demonstrates that flat surface quality which served him so expediently well in *U.S.A.* His characters, for all the individual attention paid them, are not rescued from the tendency of their author to reduce characterization to that dead level of narration which has become their author's invariable trademark.

The novels of other established authors in the 1940's show the same tendency to repeat themselves or to work persistently away at themes already worn thin. The excitement of new discoveries of talent and early successes of theme is now a memory, but the manner lingers on. In many respects, these later novels serve to emphasize the defects of execution which did exist in the early successes but were then scarcely noticed. The fiction produced by James T. Farrell, for example, reveals not much more than a shift of scene; the manner remains and its functional crudity (as of the Studs Lonigan trilogy and the O'Neill novels) is now more starkly crude and less impressive. The Bernard Clare (or Carr) series, newly begun, concerns the adventures of a young writer, transferred to New York and thus joined to the stream of activity among bohemians and intellectuals there. So far there are two novels in the series: *Bernard Clare* (1946) and *The Road Between* (1949). And there is no reason to suppose that there will not be at least two more in the series. These novels do have the opportunity of a change in setting, but it is an opportunity perhaps more unfortunate than otherwise. Farrell's portrayal of the intellectual life in New York of the twenties and thirties suffers badly from two kinds of repetition: it is itself a stale repetition of a theme already treated too often in American fiction; and it lends itself poorly to the sincere but flat persistence of Farrell's style. It is an example of the "stuck whistle" rhetoric so often seen in these latter-day renewals of an already exhausted fictional style.

Sinclair Lewis tried to keep his literary fortunes alive by means of another strategy. He changed his themes, or introduced new ones. *Kingsblood Royal* (1947) is an exploitation of the race question, given Lewis's own kind of middle-class orientation. *The God-Seeker* (1949) abandons the present, to return to a pioneer Midwest and the deep religious fervor of an un-Gantryish world. But these novels, if they prove anything, testify to the fact that a Lewis turned serious had lost much of his earlier effectiveness.

Nowhere have the pitfalls of a reiterative manner proved more disastrous than in the succession of novels published in recent years by Erskine Caldwell. *Tobacco Road* (1932) and *God's Little Acre* (1933) took advantage of that peculiarly mixed interest which characterized the 1930's audience; the poor whites of those novels were both rewardingly farcical creatures and objects of a sympathetic social interest.

Caldwell has not been able to forget them; nor has he been
able to rid himself of the mixture of the comic and pathetic
in his portrayal of them. His almost complete surrender to
the natural villainy of the preacher in *Journeyman* (1935)
had its own kind of attractiveness; but poor Spence Douthit
of *Tragic Ground* (1944) is knocked about by both his well-
intentioned friends and stereotyped social workers. Caldwell, like Steinbeck, has been victimized by a serious intellectual failure. There is no genuinely sound standard of
measurement by which the creations of either can be said
to have advanced from their initial success. During the war,
Steinbeck attempted a melodramatic variation upon the
anti-Fascist theme, in *The Moon Is Down* (1942), and failed
dismally to get even to the surface of the problem. He returned, in *Cannery Row* (1945), to the world of *Tortilla
Flat;* and in *The Wayward Bus* (1947) he showed clearly
the poverty of conception which had in greater or less degree hurt his earlier work.

All of these novels are unhappy reminders of talents that
have not proved substantial enough to survive initial success, or at least have not been improved. Much the same
criticism can be made of the most recent novel of Ernest
Hemingway, *Across the River and into the Trees* (1950).
In this novel the style, the dialogue, the military background
and setting are victims of Hemingway's self-indulgence.
Having lost the genuine relevance they once had, in *The
Sun Also Rises,* the dialogue and exposition betray an almost incredible artificiality. Colonel Cantwell's expectation
of death from heart failure forces him to plan a final sequence of pleasures; and these involve a woman (now much
younger than her hero), some pleasant waiters and bar-
tenders, much and various drink and conversation. These
are in a sense on exhibition from his earlier novels, but

none of them has any but the most specious dignity or relevance. The novel contains, in addition, a variety of observations upon contemporary military events and celebrities. One cannot overemphasize the vulgarity of this novel, its sad indication of a talent corrupted and enfeebled by the loss of aesthetic discipline.

iii

The uses to which naturalism has been put in the last decade testify to the undying vitality of that development in American fiction. In the 1940's, for the most part, naturalism has been freed of its leftist imperative; it no longer serves one or another ideological purpose. It has also assimilated the more superficial elements of psychiatric research. The influence of Dreiser, Farrell, and Hemingway is pervasive. Beyond that, the slickness of John O'Hara's conceptions has been added to the contribution made by James Cain to the surface picture of American violence.

An atmosphere of cynicism pervades this brand of American fiction. That man is corruptible and that each man has his price we need go no further than Mark Twain to discover. In the novels of the 1930's this venality was generally ascribed to a particular kind of political and moral immaturity. The men of the cities were described in those novels as victims of a remediable corruption. The world of Willard Motley's *Knock on Any Door* (1947) and Ira Wolfert's *Tucker's People* (1943) documents the corruption and disabuses us of hope of remedy. Violence and moral perversion are, in a wide range of popular naturalistic novels, not the critical beginnings of social realism but ends in themselves. There are suggestions made that we should react with proper horror to the spectacles contained therein;

we are supposed, for example, to find reasons for the evil end of Motley's Nick Romano, to pity and condemn him in equal measure. Romano has his Danny O'Neill, in the sober, conscientious brother Julian. The novel carries its intent from Dreiser (let us pity and behold) to Farrell, but it is a muddled affair of confused emotion and sentiment.

These novelists rely chiefly upon the mechanics of depravity and spiritual impoverishment. This fiction reveals the most superficial advances upon the "scientific knowledge" so proudly displayed by earlier naturalists. There is a smattering of ignorance about the minutiae of psychiatry— the behavior of various perverts and "psychos" is at times a part of the landscape, at times a crucial element in the discussion of motive. Worst of all is the slickness of appeal which this fiction makes—its pace is accelerated, its surface detail crowded, by the facts of the police court, the psychoanalyst's case-book, and the advances made in modern methods of crime detection. Superficially imposed, these portrayals have no intellectual or moral purpose; they have no purpose at all, beyond the obvious one of entertaining.

Only a few of these novels escape this naturalist impasse, and warrant attention as serious fiction. Nelson Algren's *The Man with the Golden Arm* (1949) is one of these. In this novel the best possibilities of the 1930's naturalism are realized. It is in the tradition of such American versions of the Dostoevskian "underground man" as Edward Dahlberg's *Bottom Dogs* (1930). The horror of Algren's Skid Row setting is unrelieved, but it is also not shamelessly exploited as a commodity. This is a man-made evil which man can neither understand nor control. The police are implicated along with the derelicts and petty criminals. Murder becomes not an act involving moral decision and responsibility but a circumstantial part of the novel's texture.

"Frankie Machine" goes to his death, not with the stupidly conceived grin we find on Romano's face, but in obedience to the most hapless and pathetic circumstance. For all its atmosphere of police lineups and crime, the novel is curiously static and unhurried. It is perhaps one of the best uses that can be made of a tradition which has added great bulk but little dignity to our fiction. It has at least the merits of a literary intelligence, which resists the temptation either to exploit or speciously to resolve the tensions of the world it has chosen to portray.

Such novels as Saul Bellow's *The Victim* (1947) and Paul Bowles's *The Sheltering Sky* (1949) are extensions of naturalism in that their authors provide a naturalistic surface but offer in addition a complex order of inference and meaning. Certainly Bellow's second novel—his first was *Dangling Man* (1946)—makes significant use of the materials to press for a psychological and moral meaning in the thick atmosphere of a Manhattan summer. The hero, Asa Leventhal, admits into his company, then into his apartment and his life, a man for whose dismissal from a position he had once been responsible—inadvertently responsible perhaps, but the novel's major concern is to explore the real nature of one man's moral involvement with and obligation to another. The facts of this situation are always given with an almost tortured respect for their factualness; beyond them and beneath, however, hero and author worry them into a succession of monologues of the conscience, punctuated by intermittent and awkward explosions of anger, self-pity, and shame. The *meaning* of the facts is Bellow's enduring concern: *Is* there a moral debt to be paid, and by what means can it be paid? More than that, *when* is the debt actually discharged? All of this is a gratifying advance from the amateur excursions of the early naturalists in "philosophic"

definition. Despite crudities of style and passages in which
Leventhal's moral conscientiousness is more painful than
convincing, Bellow's novel is an encouraging exercise of
the advantages made available to the novelist through several decades of naturalist fiction. It is superior also to *The
Sheltering Sky,* whose value lies chiefly in its precise rendering of Sahara sand, sky, and heat. It is perhaps proper to say
that such a world dwarfs its people, who adjust to it in
various strange ways, and this statement is most successfully
made by Bowles. The weakness of the novel is not that the
dramatic problems created by the Sahara towns and cities
are not real, but rather that the persons suffering from them
lose definition and precision—their integrity as persons is
lost. The strangeness and the extremes of natural terror
do not contribute to their meaning but rather extinguish it.
It is possible to draw an inference from all of this concerning the universal extinction of human significance, a peculiarly modern tragedy. But this is certainly going beyond
Bowles's intention—or at least beyond his achievement.

iv

For all its abundance, the fiction of the 1940's demonstrates no great advances in the art. Many of the novels discussed so far in this chapter are, in one way or another,
duplications or extensions of practices long since established. For the most part, they suffer from a continuing two-
dimensional expansion of the values of realism without
much intelligent attention to complexity. In fact, the predominating event of the decade, the war, encouraged such
an expansion at the expense of depth. In nearly every case,
the fiction gains facts but loses subtlety. The tricks of the

1930's remain a means of organizing facts, but these facts remain on the surface of event and character. The "novel of manners," as Mrs. Wharton called her principal work, does not lend itself to more than the most superficial uses in the 1940's. The inspiration is not hers, or James's, but comes from the naturalists, and from Wolfe. Even the best of Hemingway's influence scarcely results in more than an inadvertent decorum of style.

In the criticism of fiction, however, the results have been quite different. Three American novelists have enjoyed revivals of interest: Henry James, F. Scott Fitzgerald, and, more recently, Edith Wharton. In each case, the interest is as much in the manner as in the matter; indeed, the primary incentive for the interest is a curiosity over technique, an analytical concern with the interaction of means with ends. It must be admitted, however, that such an interest has helped to create, not so much new novels as more critical expositions of the old ones. Whatever its ultimate effect may be, it has at present a very limited influence upon what fiction is being published. Its most noticeable impression is revealed in the art of the short story and the novelette, as these are found published in the critical reviews. There are evidences of a careful apprenticeship in such novels as Jean Stafford's *The Mountain Lion* (1947) and Peter Taylor's *A Woman of Means* (1950). These novels have their own great merits, though it would be a mistake to compare them with the great achievements of Henry James, or even with some of the lesser accomplishment of Mrs. Wharton. Miss Stafford's study of childhood shows an excellent restraint and acuteness of perception, which serves partly to erase the unfortunate impression made by the clutter of her first novel, *Boston Adventure* (1944). Taylor's first novel has the eminent advantage of its author's practice in shorter fiction.

In a time of bulky, ambitious, and pretentious works, the brevity of *A Woman of Means* is a refreshing virtue, the more so because it is a brevity of concentration.[1] Taylor has been impressed by the need for such concentration of meaning and has brilliantly applied the technical lessons offered by a growing body of criticism. Largely the advantage is gained through a rigorous adherence to narrative point of view; the narrator is Quint Dudley, a boy of eleven at the time the events of the novel take place. Through his brilliantly sufficient, yet admirably limited, sensibility the family tragedy is observed and told. The stepmother brings two daughters into Quint's world, and tensions are developed because of the need of the two separate families to respect and love each other. To this situation is added the problem of success and the father's desire for respect. His new wife's wealth does not bring it to him; indeed, he is faced with his own failure and is forced into a number of explanations and new beginnings. The greatest drama of the novel concerns the stepmother's love of Quint, her eventual breakdown and the fantasies of self-pity and self-recrimination which precede it. There is an admirable success of tone in all of this: the events, translated by the adult narrator into the eleven-year-old point of view of himself as a child, leave a rich store of ambiguity which is appropriate to the situation itself. Reasons for action are never so clear in actuality as they appear in documentary sum-

[1] Compare it, for example, with these recent novels: Ross Lockridge's *Raintree County* (1948), Hiram Haydn's *The Time Is Noon* (1948), and John Kerouac's *The Town and the City* (1950). Each of them is excessively long, with a length that is the product either of naïveté or of self-indulgence. In the first, the technical experiments prolong the narrative without improving it; in the second, the ideational content becomes repetitious and redundant; the third suffers from a prolonged extension of egocentric detail. There is talent in every one of these novels, but in none of them a sufficient exercise of a restraining sense of limits or of the means used to derive meaning without an overbearing repetition of data.

maries. It is this genuine complexity of the meanings which pull against each other that Taylor's method has preserved. *A Woman of Means* has its own fictional equivalent of poetic excellence. It does not rant or rave; it quietly states. It does not presume a superficial power of reductive understanding; it confines its purview to the sensibility of the narrator. It is neither pompously assertive nor overwritten. It is splendidly contained and therefore aesthetically sound and unpretentious.

One may say that *A Woman of Means* is the best product we have of the recent growth of serious critical attention to the novel. That attention does not guarantee success; Taylor's gift is peculiarly adapted to the task of translating critical insight into creative work. Other writers, similarly aware of the new criticism of fiction, may not have so happy a result. Frederick Buechner's *A Long Day's Dying* (1950) is a melancholy reminder that Henry James cannot be equalled merely by being imitated. Buechner has studied James's style, has repeated it, and has all but unconsciously parodied it. The problem of the novel concerns a widow who, on a visit to her son on the campus of an Ivy League university, spends the night with a young instructor. Fearing that her affair will be discovered, she accuses the instructor of having had an unnatural relationship with her son. All of which requires an elaborate arrangement of intrigue and dialogue. The novel develops none of the implications of this plot, though it rather elaborately provides the mechanics of development: the situation leads to nothing, it merely subsides. Tristram Bone, who appears to have been intended as the *confidant,* has an identity of his own which is more interestingly given than his function is explained. Incidental scenes, often clever and effective in themselves, contribute next to nothing to the narration: the German cook's

journey to the park, for example, to scrub off the green
paint some student-vandals have splashed on a statue of
Goethe. Tristram Bone is himself a model of eccentricity:
his pet monkey, who grossly parodies human actions, gro-
tesquely kills himself when he imitates a gesture with his
master's razor. In addition, Mr. Buechner proposes to apply
the myth of Tereus and Philomela to Elizabeth's sacrifice of
her son. The novel possesses several such beginnings, but
has scarcely a meaningful development of any of them. In
view of this failure, the elaborate emulation of the Jamesian
style seems especially unfortunate and needless. One sentence should suffice as illustration:

Not only in the way Steitler [the young instructor-victim] spoke,
though it was applicable enough there—he spoke slowly, not
drawing out the words themselves but placing them at intervals
from one another, controlling the silences between sentences and
after thoughts, giving the impression of thinking ahead but not
to the sacrifice of either what he was saying at the moment or the
ease with which it was, if he so chose, possible to talk with him—
for it seemed to hold equally true, this fluency, this colloquial
ease, this particular control, in other matters as well.

Elizabeth Pollet's *A Family Romance* (1950) is less unpleasant rhetorically, as it is more successful formally. It is
written largely through the perception of children and
young persons. The title is intended to have a culminating
irony. The novel is a recounting of the tragic imbalance of
familial relationships which exists in spite of surface ap-
pearances of happiness and good feeling. It has its persuasive
virtues, but it is after all a failure in consequence of the
immaturity of view from which it is written. Taylor's point
of view was, above all, managed with the consummate skill
of the adult artist; Miss Pollet's novel appears most of the

time to have been written by the very young persons who are its principal characters.[2] In consequence, many of the scenes are hurriedly contrived; the character of Charles Lucas (who might have proved the means of externalizing the Reynolds tensions) is inadequately exploited; and the novel ends on an extremely improbable note.

Tennessee Williams' first novel, *The Roman Spring of Mrs. Stone* (1950), can perhaps also be considered here, since it is the result of a plot-situation studied out and contained. Mrs. Stone is a widow, fiftyish, who comes to Rome after years of Broadway successes, apparently to live out her days in comparative obscurity. She falls quite desperately and jealously in love with a young Italian opportunist, a *marchetta,* who is thirty years younger than she. In the rather obvious development of this theme, Mrs. Stone is turned into a jealous and wretched lover, forever suspicious, and rightly, of Paolo's sincerity, and finally left alone as he pursues a more promising opportunity. Williams provides the reader with excursions into Mrs. Stone's past—her great beauty, her cunning in protecting a star's position, her avoidance of passion for fear of its interference with her career. This tender analysis of post-forty pathos is designed to give us an assurance that Mrs. Stone is a creature to be pitied, that this is no mere sex-starved American female throwing herself away for the benefit of a cynical young Italian. A strong effort is made to underscore the pitiful character of her descent into an inferno of self-degradation. The novel fails because it succeeds only too obviously in making clear its too slender theme. Whatever there is of power in Mr. Williams' plays is strangely lacking here. The

[2] Too many recent novelists have read Henry James's *What Maisie Knew* with the false belief that Maisie's intelligence is the directive of the novel's insights; Miss Pollet should, after all, be her adult self and not Maisie. James remained himself through all variations of point of view.

style is generally stilted and awkward, sometimes amateur-
ishly self-conscious: "She knew that she, too, had once had
beauty like that and had enjoyed the anarchistic privileges
of such beauty but that her license to enjoy them had been
revoked by the passage of time."

A major and as yet scarcely touched theme of the 1940's
is the problem of the political and moral sensibility awkwardly placed in a world where oversimplification is common. The burden inherited by the sensitive liberal who
has outlived the pertinence of his naïvely held principles is
a remarkably rewarding subject for the novelist. To give it
successful treatment requires a subtle balance of knowledge
and insight. Perhaps only one American novelist has had the
intelligence and the courage to manage it properly. Lionel
Trilling's *The Middle of the Journey* (1947) is the best
novel of this genre we have yet seen. It does not offer the
subtlety of analysis that is evident in his short story, "The
Other Margaret," but it approaches a difficult set of narrative themes with remarkable intelligence and insight. John
Laskell, the protagonist of Trilling's novel, has reached a
critical middle point in his "journey." After an illness during which he has at times approached death, and even in-
dulgently wished it, Laskell visits his friends, the Crooms,
in Connecticut for the summer.[3] Because of his prolonged
illness, with its enforced separation from the society of his
friends, interests, and work, he is able to view all of these
with some detachment. The novel is largely an account of

[3] The wish for death is highly significant; in feeling it, Laskell expresses
the most poignant criticism of the liberal's "life-drive." This is at least what
Trilling intends: the death wish has been forgotten in the climactic effort
of the 1930's to make the world a tensely real utopia of things and securities;
in such a world, no attention can conveniently be paid the metaphysical inferences made for centuries from the facts of human imperfection. When
Laskell suffers a dreadful suspension of his rational confidence at the rail-
way station, his predicament is an ideological tragedy from which liberals
might make thoughtful inferences.

Laskell's revaluation of the 1930's political mind. During the stay he notes both the pathos and the dangers of the liberal mind and imagination, as these are demonstrated by Nancy and Arthur Croom. The views to which Laskell had previously subscribed with some vigor of conviction now seem harmful or at least unfortunate stereotypes. For one thing, they lead to Nancy's false admiration for "Duck" Caldwell, whom she mistakenly takes for a representative common man. Duck's indifference and irresponsibility, his drinking and his vulgarity, are all excused and even admired as extenuating virtues. Nancy also views narrowly what she regards as the cowardly desertion by Gifford Maxim of "the Party"; in leaving the Party, Maxim has expressed contempt for one of her most cherished illusions; in speaking and writing of the moral burden of society, he has upset her views by reintroducing a Christian issue into them and thus complicating them. In short Nancy is herself a pattern of the liberal's oversimplification of all social and moral values; in her one-sided evaluation of all those who doubt or differ, she underscores the liberal fallacy of seeking moral and intellectual "purity" at the expense of truth and integrity. Laskell's growing awareness of all of this is accompanied by a developing tension between him and his old friends. The novel is largely a commentary upon the false center of liberal conviction from which so many wrong-headed and futile gestures had proceeded in the decade. Trilling wishes in it not only to point to the danger of this conviction but also to restore—in the person of Laskell—to the modern intelligence some of the complexity which a too facile reading of human nature had discarded. In all of this he succeeds admirably; as a fictional enlargement of an intellectual crisis peculiar to the 1930's, *The Middle of the Journey* is a great contribution to a fundamental awareness of that decade's intellectual and emotional deficiencies.

The novels of Robert Penn Warren are more ambitious, wider in the scope of their materials, and less limited in purview by recent or immediate concerns. The novels are concerned largely with the progress of the individual conscience in a world and society which both disillusions and corrupts. His protagonists or narrators generally begin with a simple, abstract view of virtue and of soul. Their experiences tax that view heavily, if they do not entirely discredit it; and it is not unlikely that the view will eventually serve not as a deterrent to but as a rationalization of evil. What Robert Heilman describes as the theme of *World Enough and Time* (1950) can with some modification be applied as well to his other novels: Warren's theme is "the failure of a private, subjective 'ideal' realm to come to terms with, to be integrated with, to be married to a realm of public life and activity, the realm of politics and society and group action, of law and justice."[4] Especially in his most recent novel and in its predecessor, *All the King's Men* (1946), this theme is developed with a full awareness that the evil done by his heroes is not simply the consequence of their having entered public life, but rather may also have been implicit in the ideal before experience sets in. The evil resident in the protagonist is in large part a failure on his part to define clearly his own motives, to separate the selfish from the ideal, and to accommodate himself to the particulars of the world which qualify the ideal and require redefinition. The evil is also the consequence of naïveté regarding human affairs— a failure to find a middle ground between idealism and cynicism. In large part this view is also related to two contrasting interpretations of modern society; Warren shares

[4] See "Tangled Web," *Sewanee Review*, Winter 1951, pp. 107–19.

the Agrarian argument for a necessary tradition which understands the land and those who live on and by it, and this belief has influenced his criticism of modern drives for political and economic power. In the tragic disintegration of Percy Munn's ideal, in *Night Rider* (1939), Warren sees the basic confusion of his hero's purpose, his eventual single obsession with violent means to achieve a narrowly conceived end. At the beginning, Munn's life promises a peaceful law career, a simple orderly life. Through appeals made to his conscience and to his "moral view," he is drawn more and more deeply into the affairs of the Tobacco Co-operative, at war with the tobacco interests. Violence, at first a cautiously used defensive measure, eventually becomes a constant necessity, and it destroys both the purpose of the organization and the balance of Munn's intention and motive. The tendency of the desire for power to override all conscience and caution is seen in another context in *At Heaven's Gate* (1943), especially in the contrast between Bogan Murdock, the man of wealth and power, and Ashby Wyndham, whose simple observations on religion and morality counterpoint Murdock's restless and unhappy drive for an increase of wealth and power.[5]

The last two novels bear even more heavily upon this preoccupation. Willie Stark of *All the King's Men* is at first a simple man of the land, whose views of political integrity are rigorously pure. When he first discovers that he is being used by the state machine, he awakens to his responsibility and fights for his own ideal. Very soon, however, he loses sight of it and is overcome by the love of power and influence over his people. He pitifully holds on to the earlier

[5] This counterpoint is the novel's greatest value, as it is a symptom of its genuine weakness. In the reprint of the novel, poor Wyndham was omitted.

motive, develops his own explanation of political corruption and gangsterism, and tries to justify his acts on the ground that evil must be done so that a larger good may result. The state hospital, for which he engages Adam Stanton as director, proves the culminating crisis in Stark's career; because of it and Stanton's hatred for him, Stark is assassinated and the world he has built collapses. Warren has in this case selected a narrator, Jack Burden, in the hope that the issues will through him be clearly defined. In many ways, the use of a narrator here does provide some clarity; but Burden is after all merely a weak commentator upon the political affairs of Stark. His struggle to accept and explain Stark's successive steps toward corruption and loss of integrity provides a very slender frame for the evaluation of Stark's career; we are supposed to feel that Jack Burden's moral sensibility has been "educated" through what he sees in Stark.

World Enough and Time moves back in time to the Kentucky of the early nineteenth century. Historical setting and fact here provide enforcing and authenticating particulars for the moral struggle of Jeremiah Beaumont. Warren once more begins with a purely defined moral ideal, abstracted from actuality because of Beaumont's singleness of purpose and motive. Unlike Stark, Beaumont retains much of that purpose throughout; the novel serves as a questioning both of its purity and of its value. Throughout his experiences, Beaumont faces the compromises made in the world; the errors compounded in the world at first astonish him and then deeply involve him. His tortured journey through that world is made up of a hundred questionings and decisions qualified by doubt, misgiving, and desperate rationalization. His friends betray him (or betray his ideal), confuse and bewilder him, until he is himself forced into acts of violence which he cannot honestly understand or wholly accept. In the end, Beaumont's ideal is responsible not for a clarification of the world but for his own defeat. The world is more complex than any integrity can make it; good cannot publicly be exercised without its "contaminating" consequences. But these are only partial lessons; we are not left with moral definition but only with the disillusioning collapse of Beaumont's ideal, a collapse caused by his failure to understand the world. Beaumont as hero differs from Warren's other heroes; he is Jack Burden transformed from narrator to protagonist; he examines himself, not another, and he is in turn examined in a number of ways by others. What we finally get from all of this examination is the moral stuff of the world and of time: a complex fabric, not pure but composed of many and various materials and colors.

Trilling defines the risk of intellectual oversimplification within a limited but brilliantly seen context; Warren has, in his novels, tried to define a larger risk, to expand the context and to multiply the dangers involved in adjustment to the reality of social behavior. In undertaking such an ambitious program, Warren has drawn upon history past and present; he has made his novels large in scope, rich in detail, overflowing with documentation and metaphor. Except for *Night Rider,* his novels suffer from an embarrassment of riches, a diffusion of talents and gifts. They are largely overwritten, luxuriant rather than complex, a magnificent waste of materials and techniques. They are nevertheless first-rate testimonies of a genuine and serious artist working sincerely with his materials and unwilling to cheapen them by recourse to any of several easy or popular simplifications.

v

The novelists just now beginning to publish should certainly profit from the very real advances that the art of American fiction has made in the past half-century. However imperfect most of our novelists have proved to be, the most important of them have made a genuine contribution to the form and the significance of the modern novel. The two principal directions of that fiction have been followed with a fair consistency: the novel as an art form and the novel as social document have both been crucially advanced by means of American contributions to them. The first of these has had support from various sources: the progress of the Jamesian influence has been marked, especially in the fiction of Edith Wharton, Willa Cather, and Ellen Glasgow; but it is also seen in the special concern over form, structure, and point of view found in Faulkner's novels. The second principal kind of American fiction has undergone several changes of form and setting. More susceptible to the shifting nature of public events, the "novel of social purpose" has moved to adjust itself to the peculiar needs and pressures of society. The naturalist novel, with its vagrant applications of science and psychology, was altered considerably in the 1930's, and documentary naturalism gave way in that decade to the novel of social persuasion and political demonstration. The techniques, the use of exhaustive factual support, the formal strategies characteristic of this type of novel, have proved to be very popular for the new generation of writers, whose first novels appeared in the 1940's.

In any case, the emphatic purpose of the American novelists was to present a vision or interpretation of life, to bring to the novel a sense of immediate present reality, and to translate the idiom of the present world into the materials of an art. Though seldom ideally fulfilled, this purpose has given American fiction a distinction in modern literature. Those novelists who have most successfully learned to solve, or at least have found some way of meeting, the problems of technique associated with the form of the novel, have left a more than satisfactory record of their accomplishment. Fitzgerald, Faulkner, and Hemingway are perhaps the best of them—and, in each case, they have managed to produce works of an impressive merit and stature. No novel of the last ten years has succeeded quite so well as *The Great Gatsby, The Sun Also Rises, The Sound and the Fury,* or *Absalom, Absalom!* Nor have the best achievements of Henry James and Edith Wharton been equaled. But there is no doubt that all of these works, and many others, have provided both example and challenge enough for the novelists of the immediate future.

There is no reason to believe that the flood of naturalist novels should continue unabated in the future, save for the very real one that they have "caught on" with the public and now often outsell historical romances. The opportunities for the writing of good fiction now seem even greater than they ever were before. The development of a proper critical approach to the novel has been slow; most of the really good critical studies and textbooks have been largely confined to the short story. But we are no longer in a position where we need refer to Henry James as our only serious critical student of the art. If the novelist can take advantage of the all-too-well-established reputation of the naturalist mode without suffering from the weaknesses of discipline which seem to accompany it, he will most certainly be able to use it to his credit. He should also be able to preserve his talent from the temptations which often wrecked Fitzgerald's art—those which seem to make a novel slick and superficial and reduce the value of an intrinsically sound conception. There is little likelihood that the first-rate novels of the next decade will be written by men who produced the good work of the past. They will come, perhaps, from new American writers, who have been trained and disciplined and who have both something to say and a clear notion of the best means of saying it.

A SELECTED BIBLIOGRAPHY

I. THE MODERN AMERICAN NOVEL

Beach, Joseph Warren, *American Fiction, 1920–1940*. New York, Macmillan Co., 1941.
———. *The Outlook for American Prose*. Chicago, University Press, 1926.
———. *The Twentieth-Century Novel: Studies in Technique*. New York, Century Co., 1932.
Boynton, Percy H. *America in Contemporary Fiction*. Chicago, University Press, 1940.
Burgum, Edwin Berry. *The Novel and the World's Dilemma*. New York, Oxford University Press, 1947.
Cargill, Oscar. *Intellectual America: Ideas on the March*. New York, Macmillan Co., 1941.
Cowley, Malcolm (ed.). *After the Genteel Tradition: American Writers Since 1910*. New York, W. W. Norton and Co., 1937.
Frohock, Wilbur M. *The Novel of Violence in America: 1920–1950*. Dallas, The University Press, 1950.
Geismar, Maxwell. *The Last of the Provincials: The American Novel, 1915–1925*. Boston, Houghton Mifflin Co., 1947.
———. *Writers in Crisis: The American Novel between Two Wars*. Boston, Houghton Mifflin Co., 1942.

Hartwick, Harry. *The Foreground of American Fiction*. New York, American Book Co., 1934.

Hatcher, Harlan H. *Creating the Modern American Novel*. New York, Farrar and Rinehart, Inc., 1935.

Kazin, Alfred. *On Native Grounds*. New York, Reynal and Hitchcock, 1942.

Lewis, Wyndham. *Men without Art*. London, Cassell and Co., 1934.

Magny, Claude-Edmonde. *L'Age du roman americain*. Paris, Editions du Seuil, 1948.

Monroe, N. Elizabeth. *The Novel and Society*. Chapel Hill, University of North Carolina Press, 1941.

Muller, Herbert J. *Modern Fiction: A Study of Values*. New York, Funk and Wagnalls Co., 1937.

O'Connor, William Van (ed.). *Forms of Modern Fiction*. Minneapolis, University of Minnesota Press, 1948.

Snell, George D. *The Shapers of American Fiction, 1798–1947*. New York, E. P. Dutton and Co., 1947.

Trilling, Lionel. *The Liberal Imagination*. New York, Viking Press, 1950.

Van Doren, Carl C. *Contemporary American Novelists, 1900–1920*. Revised and enlarged edition. New York, Macmillan Co., 1940.

Whipple, Thomas K. *Spokesmen: Modern Writers and American Life*. New York, D. Appleton and Co., 1928.

Wilson, Edmund. *The Boys in the Back Room*. San Francisco, The Colt Press, 1941.

II. THE CRAFT OF FICTION

Ames, Van Meter. *Aesthetics of the Novel*. Chicago, University Press, 1928.

Anderson, Sherwood. *The Modern Writer*. San Francisco, Lantern Press, 1925.

Bentley, Phyllis E. *Some Observations on the Art of Narrative*. New York, Macmillan Co., 1947.

Brooks, Cleanth and Robert Penn Warren (eds.). *Understanding Fiction*. New York, F. S. Crofts and Co., 1943.

Cather, Willa. *On Writing*. New York, Alfred A. Knopf, Inc., 1949.

Comfort, Alex. *The Novel and Our Time*. Letchworth, Hertfordshire, England, Phoenix House, 1948.

DeVoto, Bernard A. *The World of Fiction*. Boston, Houghton Mifflin Co., 1950.

Dobrée, Bonamy. *Modern Prose Style*. Oxford, University Press, 1934.

Drew, Elizabeth A. *The Modern Novel*. New York, Harcourt, Brace and Co., 1926.

Forster, E. M. *Aspects of the Novel*. New York, Harcourt, Brace and Co., 1927.

Glasgow, Ellen. *A Certain Measure*. New York, Harcourt, Brace and Co., 1943.

Gordon, Caroline, and Allen Tate (eds.). *The House of Fiction*. New York, Charles Scribner's Sons, 1950.

Grabo, Carl H. *The Technique of the Novel*. New York, Charles Scribner's Sons, 1928.

James Henry. *The Art of Fiction and Other Essays*. With an Introduction by Morris Roberts. New York, Oxford University Press, 1948.

————. *The Art of the Novel*, ed. Richard P. Blackmur. New York, Charles Scribner's Sons, 1934.

Liddell, Robert. *A Treatise on the Novel*. London, Jonathan Cape, 1947.

Lubbock, Percy. *The Craft of Fiction*. Reprint edition. New York, Peter Smith, 1945. (Original edition, 1921).

McHugh, Vincent. *Primer of the Novel.* New York, Random House, Inc., 1950.

Muir, Edwin. *The Structure of the Novel.* New York, Harcourt, Brace and Co., 1929.

Ortega y Gasset, José. *The Dehumanization of Art; and Notes on the Novel.* Translated by Helene Weyl. Princeton, University Press, 1948.

Orvis, Mary Burchard. *The Art of Writing Fiction.* New York, Prentice-Hall, Inc., 1948.

Pritchett, Victor S. *The Living Novel.* New York, Reynal and Hitchcock, 1947.

Roberts, Morris. *Henry James's Criticism.* Cambridge, Harvard University Press, 1929.

Schorer, Mark (ed.). *The Story: A Critical Anthology.* New York, Prentice-Hall, Inc., 1950.

West, Ray B. and R. W. Stallman (eds.). *The Art of Modern Fiction.* New York, Rinehart and Co., 1949.

Wharton, Edith. *The Writing of Fiction.* New York, Charles Scribner's Sons, 1925.

INDEX